A BASIC APPROACH
to
EXECUTIVE
DECISION MAKING

A BASIC APPROACH to EXECUTIVE DECISION MAKING

Alfred R. Oxenfeldt
David W. Miller
Roger A. Dickinson

 A Division of American Management Associations

The figure on p. 170 of this book is reprinted by permission of Synectics, Inc.
Copyright © 1964 by Synectics, Inc. All rights reserved.

Library of Congress Cataloging in Publication Data

Oxenfeldt, Alfred Richard, 1917-
  A basic approach to executive decision making.

  Includes index.
  1. Decision-making. I. Miller, David Wendell,
joint author. II. Dickinson, Roger A., joint author.
III. Title.
HD30.23.O93   658.4'03   78-1361
ISBN 0-8144-5467-4

Second Printing

PREFACE

The field of decision making is vast; it ranges from analyses of the functioning of the unconscious to cookbook recipes on steps in decision making. One can distinguish at least the following major divisions of the subject: the processing of information for decision-making purposes; the most effective sequence in which the subdecisions involved in decision should be made; how decisions are made in fact, with emphasis on the most common errors; how decisions should be approached (prescription rather than description); and a detailed analysis of individual aspects (for example, objectives, creativity, decision rules, or the development of rating scales) of decision making.

Decision making is also important. Executives are continuously making decisions that affect the futures of many. One educator made this statement:

> In this tense, ever more crowded, ever more interdependent world, decision making is becoming more and more crucial. I do

not hesitate to proclaim that the future of the human race will depend on whether our graduates, citizens of the greatest democracy on earth, members of the most highly developed technological society in the world, have the wisdom and the courage to make, and to carry out, the right decisions.*

Writings on decision making differ mainly in their fundamental orientation. A major body of writings and research on decision making is mathematical and statistical in orientation and constitutes the field of statistical decision theory. A large part of the literature is primarily psychological and deals mainly with the functioning of the brain, the nature of intuition, and the way in which decisions are distorted by humans. Writings about decisions also come from the diverse fields of politics, consumer choice, and military affairs. Many of the works in these different fields mainly describe how decisions are made; others emphasize how they ought to be made.

Our approach is primarily prescriptive; it aims to help executives perform better as decision makers. It is oriented to persons assuming job responsibilities that revolve around decision making and accepts the severe limitations of time and financial resources available for decisions, the inaccessibility of information and the unreliability of available data, the unwillingness of colleagues to cooperate, and the strong influence of preconceptions and prejudice. Above all, it accepts the great uncertainty that surrounds almost every aspect of the decision. In short, we will be concerned with executive decisions in real life rather than with the way we would like life's decisions to be.

This book aims to present a process of decision making. We look at the executive as a manager of a "decision factory."

* Jean Mayer, President of Tufts University, *The Chronicle of Higher Education,* November 8, 1976, p.32.

Indeed, in certain instances the individual decision becomes a by-product of the production line process. In the course of developing this idea, we present methods of carrying out the individual steps in decision making and consider the underlying rationale for each step.

The book was conceived by Oxenfeldt and Miller as an outgrowth of courses taught at the Columbia Graduate School of Business. They lectured on the subject together to business groups in the United Kingdom, the United States, and Canada, extending and modifying their views in response to the questions, criticisms, suggestions, and problems raised by executives.

Surprisingly, their views of and approaches to decision making are essentially identical, despite their extremely different orientations. Oxenfeldt is fundamentally an economic theorist who has specialized in marketing problems, whereas Miller is basically a mathematician who has specialized in statistics and operations research. Oxenfeldt's students include a large proportion who try to escape from teachers with a strong mathematical orientation, whereas Miller's are largely those with a deep interest and competence in mathematical approaches to business problems.

The similarity of approach did not result from the collaboration but preceded it. Indeed, in assigning initial responsibility for individual chapters, the following decision rule was adopted: the person with least prior specialized interest in the field was to assume responsibility for it. As a result, for example, Miller did not write the chapter on "models," even though he has been teaching courses in model building. Conversely, even though signaling systems and agenda decisions represent Oxenfeldt's pet notions, the materials on those subjects were initially prepared by Miller.

Roger Dickinson developed and organized the materials. Kris Anundsen edited the manuscript.

We wish to acknowledge the help and suggestions we received from many people in the course of preparing this book. In particular, we owe thanks to Ernest M. Miller, Jonathan Schwartz, Jay Shaffer, and L. Scott Miller for helpful comments and criticisms.

Alfred R. Oxenfeldt
David W. Miller
Roger A. Dickinson

CONTENTS

1

The COMPLEXITY of EXECUTIVE DECISION MAKING

A well-known management consultant was once heard to remark that a truly effective executive spends very little time making decisions. The implication was that once you have a good decision-making system, a good step-by-step procedure (computerized wherever possible), decisions will be pretty much automatic, and you can dust off your hands and turn your attention to the "action" parts of your job.

Certainly, executives are not decision makers only, but their success often depends on their decision-making skills.

Consider the variety of decisions a manager has to make. There are decisions that are repetitive and based on objective data or standard operating procedures; there are those that involve new situations where data are scanty or even nonexistent. There are decisions whose outcome is almost predictable and decisions whose outcome is a wild guess. There are tactical decisions that have to be made under severe time pressure (a situation sometimes referred to as "fighting fires") and strategic decisions based on numerous factors, with ample time to assemble and analyze the data.

There are problem-solving decisions and future-planning decisions. There are decisions involving a choice between two options and decisions involving many options. There are decisions with easily quantifiable parameters, such as money, and those whose main elements (such as social welfare or morale) are difficult to quantify. And so on. Perhaps the most persistent and crucial decisions that managers make are those concerning what is to be decided and how to allocate their time appropriately.

The amount of time that executives must devote to decision making typically increases as they move up the managerial ladder. Top executives are usually expected to devote the largest proportion of their time to decision making, and their performance is evaluated according to how well their decisions turn out. So it is not surprising that decision making has become a discipline in its own right, an important object of study and analysis. Decision making, which not only can incorporate the most sophisticated mathematical techniques but also can involve the highest forms of mental process, is a science that embodies generous quantities of art.

The process by which one arrives at a decision is complex; in fact, no one process can be applied to all decisions. Ask 25 managers, consultants, and professors of management to list the steps in the decision process, and you will probably get 25 different lists. These will have many elements in common, but they will also contain several differing elements and many that are not in the same sequence.

In this book you will find the decision process discussed in what could be considered a logical sequence of steps; however, in many types of decisions, these steps come in different orders, overlap, or are merely skimmed over. For example, model building is often the first step, occurring even before you are aware that a decision has to be made; the picture in your mind that describes the current situation is in a sense a model. And a certain amount of forecasting goes into many early stages of a decision—including the decision to make a decision.

Since decision making is so highly complex, executives are quite fallible as decision makers. Even with all the sophisticated mathematical and computer aids that have been developed in recent decades to aid the decision maker, the validity of business decisions has not increased perceptively. Human factors still get into the works and confuse things; the environment has become more volatile; competitors are smarter.

This does not, however, mean that decision making is a process that cannot be improved. The performance of most executives as decision makers can be substantially upgraded if they master a systematic approach to decision—one that permits them to make better use of what they know and to use the assistance of others effectively. Further, by just being aware of the decision process and of their own decision-making style and approaches, they will be able to avoid some common errors and pitfalls.

Over the decades, decision-making methods have evolved from primitive to supersophisticated. We can, somewhat arbitrarily, distinguish four stages in the development of this science/art: the instinctive approach, the traditional approach, the commonsense approach, and the scientific method.

The Instinctive Approach

The first and oldest kind of decision making can be called instinctive. It characterizes the decision making of animals and perhaps of primitive man. Animals employ a good deal of automatic, instantaneous, preprogrammed behavior. Bees constructing their honeycombs, beavers engineering their dams, birds building their nests are some of the countless examples of instinctive decision making.

These examples suggest that the instinctive approach — which lacks conscious, rational thought processes — is of little relevance to contemporary man. Yet all of us still have an apparatus for instinctive decision making, and it is used with reasonable frequency. Whenever a sudden, unexpected threat to life or limb arises, our instinctive decision-making equipment takes over. If it did not, few people would experience old age.

When the driver's car starts to skid on an icy road or when a rung breaks on a high ladder, there is no time for a considered decision. Survival depends on an immediate response, and only an instinctive decision will be fast enough to be useful. Because such emergency situations do arise, instinctive decision making still plays an important role in our lives, though rarely in our business decisions.

The Traditional Approach

The kind of decision making that came second in the historical development can be called traditional. This type characterizes most primitive societies today and apparently predominated in most early societies. Indeed, it held undisputed sway in most parts of the world until comparatively recent times.

In tradition-dominated societies almost every possible situation that needs resolution has arisen many times before for whole generations of predecessors. Earlier decision makers worked out what had to be done in specific situations, and the contemporary decision maker is expected to know these "proper" courses of action and to follow them.

This approach to decision problems is usually fortified by the conviction — which may often be justified — that the old-timers really were smarter than the new generation. Again, there are many situations in contemporary life where decision making is simplified by saying, "This is the way we've always done it because this is what works best, so we'll continue to do it this way."

The Commonsense Approach

There are two distinguishing characteristics of the commonsense approach. First, the decision makers are capable of articulating most of the factors that will influence their decisions; they do not rely primarily on instinct, intuition, or tradition. They understand their decision process, at least roughly, and know why they do what they do. Second, they do not use any of the analytical approaches that can be applied to complex decision problems.

For example, a decision maker might make a simple cost/benefit analysis in which the benefits are listed on one side and the costs on the other. Without making any explicit computations, the decision maker might then say, "Obviously, the costs outweigh the benefits, so common sense says not to do it." (An example of a decision maker relying on this approach might be Chester Bowles, who is described by David Halberstam as adding up the pluses and minuses of any question and coming up with a conclusion.*)

The Scientific Method

The present stage in the evolution of decision making came about as managers in government and business began to break apart the components of what they were doing, analyze each component, and attempt to get precise answers to the questions arising in the course of these activities. This stage appears to have got under way by the end of the eighteenth century in England. One early illustration is in the in-

*The Best and the Brightest, New York: Random House, 1972, p. 69.

surance industry, where decision makers discovered that some of the questions that needed answering could be handled by mathematicians and actuaries, who were developing life tables that showed the probability that a person of a given age would die within a given time.

The extension of such scientific analyses to other industries did not proceed precipitously, but already in 1832 Charles Babbage, the first person to attempt to build a big and practical computer, prescribed the use of mathematical and scientific analysis to improve production.* And by the end of the nineteenth century the application of a scientific approach to production had made considerable headway.

During the first part of the twentieth century, the application of the scientific method to specific parts of decision problems spread rapidly; the development of quality control procedures in the 1930s is one of many examples that could be cited. However, it was not discovered until later that this method could be applied to the whole decision problem rather than to selected pieces of it.

This new approach seems to have started in the English army during the Second World War. Desperate needs dictated extreme methods, and top decision makers were willing to try anything that had some chance of success. Large groups of scientists from almost every discipline were drafted or hired and put into teams, each of which was assigned some specific problem. Originally, these problems were again pieces of decision problems, such as the optimal setting on depth bombs. But with success the tendency became to give the team an entire decision problem: How should ships defend themselves against a kamikaze attack? How should planes be used in the fight against enemy submarines?

This was the early period of operations research. Many of

---

* *On the Economy of Machinery and Manufacturers*, New York: A. M. Kelley, 1963.

the operations researchers who developed their skills during World War II believed that similar methods would work equally well in the business world, so starting about 1950 they began to teach and proselyte in management circles. Their success is evidenced by the results: there are national and international associations in OR, Ph.D.'s are given in it, and most large corporations have their own OR groups.

As we have implied, living in the scientific era of decision making doesn't mean we have left the other kinds of approach behind. Far from it. No matter how many scientific techniques are available, no matter how many clever systems have been devised, no manager's decision making is free from those more primitive approaches: instinct, tradition, and common sense. The more aware we are of this fact, the better a grasp we will have of what goes into a decision.

Requirements for Sound Decisions

The most important requirement for making sound decisions is a deep understanding of the phenomena that the decision involves. If one is selecting among, say, alternative methods of removing a brain tumor, the soundness of the decision will depend most upon the decision maker's knowledge of the anatomy and pathology of the brain. If one is selecting among alternative ways of increasing the number of retailers who will carry a firm's product line, that decision will be "good" to the extent that the decision maker understands the nature, needs, situations, and aspirations of retailers of such products. Some go as far as to say that once the details of a subject are really mastered, decisions come naturally.*

Apart from an understanding of the phenomena with which the decision is concerned, the validity of the approach

---

* One believer in this theory appears to be Jimmy Carter, according to an article in *Fortune* (August 1975, p. 210).

depends on the presence of, among other things, some or all of the following ingredients: the ability to interpret data (to turn them into "information"); the ability to draw operational conclusions from data; imagination; objectivity; patience; and intuition.

It should never be assumed that sound decisions will always result from using proper procedures. After carrying out the best procedures, the final ingredient for the decision maker to add is judgment. And judgment is influenced by factors peculiar to the individual and to the organization, such as previous personal experience, preferences, assumptions, subtle or not-so-subtle group pressures, authority structures, rewards for high-risk versus low-risk decisions, and so forth.

Suppose, for example, that an executive is deciding which of two machine systems to buy. One is made by Company A, the leader in its field, and the other is made by a little-known manufacturer, Company B. After adding up the dollars and cents and figuring in the service potential and requirements, the executive determines that the machine manufactured by Company B is really better for his purposes. However, he recognizes that the other model is the "safer" choice, because if it doesn't work out, his boss will blame Company A, whereas if he buys Company B's machine and something goes wrong, his boss—a conservative type—can blame him for not buying the "best."

Also, suppose that part of the cost information on which his decision must be based comes from a colleague named Jim, whom he likes and trusts and who is also popular with his colleagues. Before our executive has even taken a glance at Jim's reports, he is predisposed to accept them, and if he sees something in the reports that doesn't quite jibe, he is likely, in view of his confidence in Jim and his own preference, to ignore the contradiction. These are just a few of the things that can weaken our executive's decision-making process.

Still, explicit procedures are a valuable help to the managerial decision maker. Although we place great value on personal experience and natural aptitude as a basis for valid decisions, these qualities are not sufficient to ensure good choices. Managers are faced with the problem of too much inconclusive information and not enough conclusive information; they are dealing with complex phenomena in a volatile environment. They must constantly handle conflict of one sort or another with colleagues; they must reckon with the actions of rival firms. They are human and fallible and subject to emotional disruption. Clearly, in today's fast-paced and complex world, they need some kind of system for creating order in decision making.

Perhaps you know highly experienced executives who can apparently arrive at reasonable and intelligent decisions without going through any "procedure." However, although they may *appear* to be operating in a seat-of-the-pants fashion, the odds are that they are following "steps" that they long ago incorporated into their intuitive approach.

A Production Line of Decisions

We suggest that executives should consider themselves primarily manufacturers of decisions. They manage resources of many kinds: a plant (space), personnel, equipment, liquid assets, and information. They engineer their facilities and procedures carefully to create a highly efficient production process. Their "factories" contain several "production lines," each one producing decisions of different magnitude, with different product features and of dissimilar quality; some are produced far more quickly and cheaply than others.

The executive is the one who is mainly responsible for establishing the various production lines; in addition, he or she picks and trains key personnel to work efficiently within the decision factory, assigns jobs to the different production lines, sets schedules, and monitors the process.

The executive will view the plant personnel primarily as a portfolio of skills that are combined with the factory to produce the output of satisfactory decisions. One element in the portfolio will be a quality-assurance person — someone who can argue in complete safety with the executive and with other managers in the decision factory. Ordinarily, the executive would keep a staff of specialists in data gathering, data interpretation, report writing, and production of creative ideas.

The executive's job is fundamentally that of a manager, rather than a doer, of decision making. The task of this person is to see that decisions of the right kind are made in the most efficient manner; they must not be overdesigned and thus become excessively costly. Among the manager's concerns are that the factory be used close to full capacity and that burdens be spread fairly evenly over the various production lines and employees.

The executive usually assigns tasks to production lines and generally sets special specifications, where required. He or she almost invariably makes a personal inspection of the final "product."

The employees know what is expected of them, without particular instruction. They know how their production line manufactures its decisions, they become experts in particular processes, and as they become more experienced in doing the job, they propose improvements in the process.

In this view of the executive as a decision maker, decisions are the output of a carefully engineered cooperative process. The executive's role is primary and dominant. However, the process of decision production should work pretty well in the executive's absence for a substantial period, and a successor should find it relatively easy to keep it operating efficiently.

Our task, then, will be to formulate a procedure for decision production that will serve executives effectively. In doing this, however, we must bear in mind that:

- There is no one process by which all decisions are made.
- The steps in almost any decision process overlap.
- Personal and unconscious factors influence decisions, sometimes crucially.
- Depending on logic alone can get you into trouble.

Also, it is important to remember that decision making permeates every aspect of the executive's total function and thus cannot be considered a discrete process standing apart from other responsibilities. Therefore, we will be giving less attention in this book to scientific or mathematical techniques (most of which are usually delegated to a technical decision specialist anyway) than to the mental activity that goes into the decision-production process.

Finally, since decision making is so often linked to problem solving (sometimes little distinction is made between the two processes), we will focus more on problem decisions than on opportunity decisions or planning decisions. But naturally that does not mean that we discount the importance of planning or of seizing opportunities.

To illustrate some of the factors that must be considered in the decision process, let us look at an incident that is typical of what happens in many organizations. This example involves a problem decision; although other examples will be given during the course of the book, we will carry this particular problem decision through various discussions in order to provide continuity.

THE MILWAUKEE PROBLEM

The vice president of marketing of a large appliance manufacturing company (Company A) has been notified that sales in one important metropolitan market have been below the expected level for two quarters in succession. Although the firm's sales were slightly higher for the nation as a whole in those quarters than in the previous year, in that one market they are down 10 percent and 25 percent as compared to sales for the same quarters in the preceding year.

When he asks what has been done to correct the situation, he learns that the regional sales manager in the affected territory—one of the best managers in the organization—is well aware of what is transpiring and thinks he knows the explanation for the difficulty. However, he is not able to prescribe a sure fire cure. Indeed, he predicts that sales will be down again in the current quarter.

The vice president of marketing is most upset with this state of affairs. His first impulse is to go straight to the site of the problem, which would require revising his busy schedule of appointments, some fairly pressing.

Here is an opportunity for the VP to make a number of decisions, not the least of which is how to spend his time in the most productive way (we will call this an "agenda decision").

Like other top-level executives, this VP is in charge of a "decision factory" and therefore is responsible for the output (ideas and solutions) of many subordinates as well as for his own output. He needs to keep on top of the entire production process and to make sure the machinery is in working order.

The details of the decision process required for such a situation will not be discussed here. But as we will see in the following chapters, the executive requires clear objectives (Chapter 2), valid models (Chapter 3), and an appropriate signaling system (Chapter 4) that indicates when action should be taken; he must know how these elements bear on his agenda decision (Chapter 5); and he must understand how they help identify the causes of the problem (Chapter 6) and possible solutions (Chapter 7). The quality of the final "product" — the chosen course of action — will depend on the appropriateness of the "decision machinery" (including forecasting tools, discussed in Chapter 8); and the efficiency of the decision-making process will depend on all these things plus the way the decision factory is organized to enhance such vital factors as creativity (Chapter 9).

2
BUSINESS OBJECTIVES

Just as road signs are of little or no value unless you know where you are driving, a decision cannot generally take you where you want to get unless you know what your goals are. Without a knowledge of objectives, a decision maker's choices are unlikely to be useful. Objectives are—or ought to be—integral to the organization's entire decision process. As an enterprise evolves over time, its objectives are constantly changing, and the executive decision process must be flexible enough to take account of these changes.

Carefully stated objectives can give clear direction to all members of an organization. The key term here is "carefully stated." Many organizations give insufficient attention to the need for making objectives explicit. One result is internal conflict and confusion caused by faulty communications. Whether goals are formulated by fiat or in a management-by-objectives system, good decision making requires that they be understood and pursued by all managers in the organization.

A mistaken view of objectives can create many problems.

During World War II, Allied losses of freighters carrying munitions to the USSR were enormous. In addition to the losses due to submarines, many of the ships were sunk by planes. To protect the ships, freighters were equipped with five-inch cannons and gunnery crews.

After a period, a study was made of the experience of ships with guns. It was found that these ships shot down almost no planes and sank no submarines. As a result, it was proposed that the guns be transferred ashore where they were badly needed.

Here, a faulty view of objectives almost resulted in serious error. Further analysis of the data showed that the rate of sinking among armed freighters was substantially lower than that of unarmed ships. Although the guns did not shoot down planes or sink subs, they helped keep both at a distance, where they were far less effective.

The decision was made to continue to arm freighters. Guns were put aboard freighters, not to shoot down planes or sink subs, but to reduce sinkings of the freighters themselves — which was the original objective that led to arming of the ships.

Certain difficulties are inherent in setting and communicating objectives:

- People and organizations ordinarily pursue many objectives rather than a single one. Indeed, it is difficult to recognize all the objectives one should pursue.
- Objectives often conflict; for example, short-term objectives often differ from long-term objectives.
- Objectives vary as to "level"; failure to separate different levels of objectives often leads to mistaken decisions.

In considering how to relate objectives to decisions, let us elaborate on the last point.

Certain goals are "ultimate." These are goals which, when

one tries to justify them, lead to the answer that "I just want them." That is, they tend to be based on subjective preferences. Other goals are instrumental; they help in the achievement of ultimate goals. We want to do well at our jobs or our studies, for example, in order to gain financial and ego rewards. These, in turn, will help us achieve ultimate goals of power and prestige and the pleasure of accomplishment.

Let us assume that a firm has unambiguously identified the ultimate objectives that management should pursue: survival, long-term profits, and growth. This statement of ultimate goals does not nearly meet the needs of the firm's decision makers for direction and guidance in selecting among alternatives. Most managers' decisions have only an indirect and unclear relationship to the firm's ultimate objectives. It is always useful, and usually essential, for *intervening* levels of objectives to be identified as well.

Given the ultimate goals stated above, the executive responsible for advertising presumably should pursue objectives involving such factors as the desired brand image, the number of reader-viewers of the desired type, the prestige of media, and the kind of information to be transmitted to specified numbers of potential customers. These are valid goals in the sense that they contribute to the firm's profitability, survival, and growth by enhancing advertising effectiveness. In short, between decisions about advertising media and ultimate objectives, one finds several intervening levels of objectives. If they are explicitly stated (see Figure 1), such intervening objectives give valuable guidance to executives who make selections among alternatives.

Firms can pursue profits, survival, and growth by many diverse means. It is highly unlikely that any two organizations would choose exactly the same intervening goals, even if their ultimate objectives were identical. *A firm's intervening goals basically reflect its strategy.* Its selection of particular intervening goals will be based on an assessment of its capabilities, resources, and opportunities, as well as on its "schemes" and bright ideas for their exploitation. It will, or should, seek

Figure 1. Ultimate goals and intervening objectives.

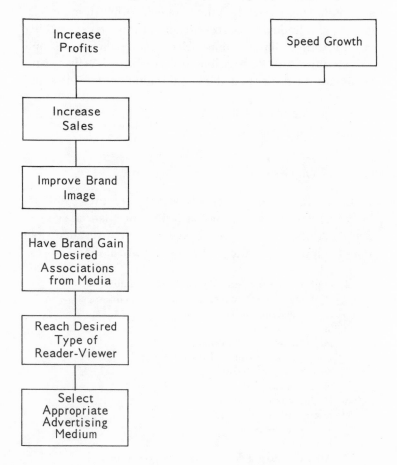

profits, survival, and growth (if those are its ultimate goals) by means that capitalize on the capabilities that it possesses rather than by means requiring skills that it lacks and cannot obtain. That is, it should seek to lead from its strengths and avoid its weaknesses.

Sometimes the means by which a firm pursues its ultimate goals are compatible with one another, and sometimes they are conflicting. Even when they are compatible, they usually compete for limited resources, so a firm cannot try everything at once without limit; it must select among alternatives and balance their use. Its decisions presumably will reflect management's assessment of the organization's capabilities and opportunities.

Let us now illustrate the three difficulties in setting and communicating objectives that we suggested earlier.

Many Objectives

Listed below are fifteen financial objectives (not all-inclusive) that some firms use as indices of financial success; firms will often try to select that action or investment that rates highest when evaluated by one or more of these indices.

1. High long-term appreciation in stock values.
2. High short-term appreciation in stock values.
3. High dividend disbursements.
4. Stable dividends.
5. High return on investment.
6. High present value of future income.
7. Favorable financial statements.
8. High net income.
9. High return on assets.
10. High return on sales.
11. Ability to borrow.
12. Liquidity.
13. Ability to float a stock issue at attractive prices.

14. Freedom from financial constraints.
15. High earnings per share.

As one would expect, some of the objectives overlap and may seem similar; however, they are different, and actions that result in an increase in one area often will produce a decrease in one or more of the others. Some of these measures of financial success are expressed in absolute dollar amounts; others are ratios. Some concern items as they appear on a firm's financial statements; others involve estimates of future earnings. Some are built on traditional accounting information; others call for estimates of "true" cost; and still others reflect a change in the firm's internal resources. Little wonder that they do not all vary together and by the same degree.

Objectives in Conflict

One can readily see that these financial objectives may conflict. Clearly, a firm's earnings per share might be increased by taking substantial long-term loans at 8 percent and earning 9 percent on that money. Certain theories of finance would suggest that the price-earnings ratio of such a firm might diminish and indeed, under certain conditions, lower the stock prices of the firm. Further, a heavy investment in long-term research would under most conditions lower short-term earnings. Effectively directed, such expenditures would presumably increase earnings in the long term. Additionally, certain patterns of earnings may be preferred by investors in the stock market because they indicate growth, yet such growth patterns are not considered by the criterion of net present value of future income.

What we must now do is examine the relative importance of each objective. This requires that we determine whether they are comparable and on the same level.

DIFFERENT LEVELS OF OBJECTIVES

The basis on which we will assign financial objectives to different levels is that of their means-ends relationship. *Anything that is a means for achieving something else is subordinate to it* (that is, is on a lower level). For example, if a firm frees itself from financial constraints by increasing both its ability to borrow and its liquidity, then we would place freedom from financial constraints (Objective #14) on a higher level than liquidity and ability to borrow. If size of dividends mainly determines stock values in the long run, then "high dividends" (Objective #3) is on a lower level than long-run stock values. And so on.

The financial objectives of individuals associated with a firm may vary with their relationship to a firm. People who frequently trade in a firm's stock are clearly concerned with the firm's near-term stock prices, whereas top managers are much more likely to be concerned with freedom from financial constraints (so that they can carry out the programs they desire) and impressive financial statements, for these will strengthen their position with the board of directors. (This does not mean that managers are not concerned with the short-term value of the firm's stock. Clearly, if management wanted to float a new issue of common stock, the market price would be very important.)

In order to simplfy the discussion, we will view the financial objectives of one group: stockholders interested in holding their stock in a firm (the ABC Company) for a long time. Here, two major questions must be answered. First, what are the main financial goals of these people? Second, are these goals all on the same level?

Stockholders holding their securities for a long-term gain will be mainly interested in long-term appreciation in stock values (Objective #1), high dividend disbursements (Objective #3), and stability of dividends (Objective #4). (In addition, they will desire that the stock they own be actively traded so that they could, in an emergency, liquidate their holdings without being forced to accept substantially less than the securities are worth. This objective, like several others, was not included explicitly in our list, although it may be subsumed under short-term appreciation of stock values.)

We shall now sort out the objectives listed earlier from the standpoint of owners of securities who seek long-term gains in the form of both stock appreciation and dividends. The most useful device for this purpose is the hierarchy, a notational device that shows level by physical position; items that are placed high are most important, most general, or simply closer to ultimate objectives than those that are low. One such hierarchy is presented in Figure 2.

We are less likely to err seriously with a hierarchy than if we merely list our objectives without taking account of their level. Without the hierarchy, we will treat low-level objectives as if they were as important as higher-level ones and will be confusing means with ends. Increased attainment of a low-level goal need not contribute to a higher-level goal. For example, increasing the liquidity of a firm above what it needs to finance its operations would not be of any particular value — that is, it would not add to its freedom from financial constraints.

Our hierarchy of objectives would be changed if we adopted a different group's viewpoint. Top management, owners, or stockholders who are also suppliers might have quite different objectives from those of other long-term stockholders. For example, top management's ultimate objectives may be financial security (the desire to retain high salary, bonuses, stock options, and pensions), the prestige of running a large firm, and the satisfaction of planning and implementing new projects. Speculators in a company's stock may be in-

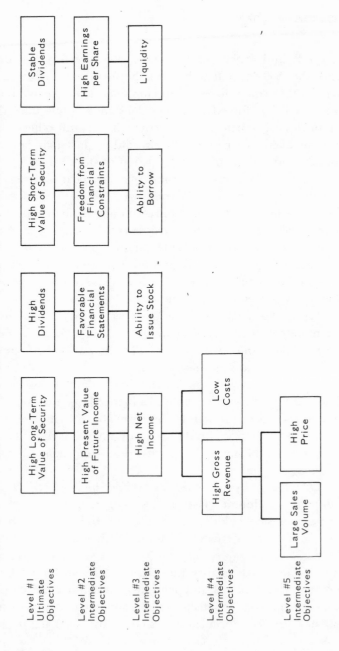

Figure 2. A possible hierarchy of financial objectives for a group of stockholders of ABC Company.

terested only in the short-term price of the common stock. A different hierarchy would be required for each of these groups.

We should stress, however, that there is no one correct version of a hierarchy. In the example discussed, some of the objectives are influenced by, and in turn have influence upon, other objectives in the hierarchy. (The reader is encouraged to identify these two-way relationships.) Therefore, a list of objectives could be arranged in more than one way — even for the same interest group, such as long-term stockholders.

AN EXAMPLE: SHORT-TERM PROFITABILITY

For the sake of brevity (but at some sacrifice of realism), let us assume that companies simply pursue the objective of short-term profitability. Short-term profitability is the difference between short-term revenues and short-term costs. To maximize short-term profits, a firm might try to maximize revenues, given some level of costs, or minimize costs, given some level of revenues. Given certain assumptions, it will normally aim for that combination of total revenues and total costs that yields the greatest total profit.

In general, management must decide whether it wishes to place particular emphasis upon expansion of revenues or contraction of costs. This decision will be based largely on its overall strategy (leading from strengths). A company that is particularly skilled in economical operation would be wise to adopt a policy of tight cost control and limited expenditure. Another firm with identical goals might stress measures to increase revenues while incurring relatively high costs, because its main strength lies in the area of demand creation.

The first company would want to consider alternative means of limiting its costs. Should it stress mechanization?

Moving to a low-cost location? Labor training? Close supervision? Use of low-cost materials? Or should it stress economies of marketing with limited expenditures on advertising, personal selling, customer service, special product features, and so forth? Or should it virtually eliminate all staff service, research, and development and employ only a few very high-caliber executives?

These alternative strategies for pursuing low costs are partly conflicting; for example, in order to achieve low costs in both manufacturing and marketing, the firm might require more rather than fewer high-caliber executives. The path chosen will reflect management's estimate of the things it can do well. If it is inefficient at marketing, it would be better off stressing its outstanding talents for efficient manufacturing and engineering by allocating managerial skills and financial resources primarily to these areas.

Consider now the other company, which wants to pursue high profitability in the short run mainly by stressing high gross revenues. It too might employ many different means to achieve its goal. It might offer highly attractive product features and appealing product design; it might advertise extensively, win the support of prestigious distributors and retailers, offer special customer services, and the like.

If it were to employ *all* of these methods of increasing revenues, its costs would be too high. To increase profitability, certain measures might be eliminated or given less financial support than others. Whether the firm elects to emphasize customer service or advertising, for example, presumably would depend on whether the company would be more effective as an advertiser or as a provider of customer service. Similarly, if it were skillful at product design or the development of innovative product features, it might rely heavily on these methods of expanding revenues and spend relatively little on alternative means that were not in its area of strength.

Constructing a Hierarchy from the Bottom

We have explored how a firm might proceed in logical steps from an initial statement of ultimate objectives to a selection of the means for pursuing these objectives. In brief, the method consists of: (1) defining the ultimate objectives, (2) identifying alternative means of pursuing the ultimate goals at intervening levels, and (3) selecting among and balancing these alternatives mainly according to what the firm does relatively well.

After establishing one level of intervening goals in this manner, a company can add other levels by repeating the process. Each of its intervening goals could be pursued by a variety of means. These varied means all represent potential intervening goals.

It is also possible, however, to construct a hierarchy of objectives by starting below the very top. A decision maker can start with very clear and accepted purposes, such as the improvement of engineering designs, more effective advertising appeals, or faster delivery from suppliers.

With such goals as starting points, one can identify higher-level objectives by asking, "Why do I want that?" The answer might be, "I want better engineering design so I can reduce manufacturing difficulties and overcome some product defects. Reducing manufacturing difficulties in turn would speed production, reduce risk of loss, and permit the use of less skilled personnel. If we overcome product defects we might achieve greater customer and reseller satisfaction, which would lead to greater customer loyalty and wider distribution and therefore to greater sales revenues." This bottom-up view of objectives is depicted in Figure 3.

Executives can start this process at many points. By so doing, they will develop many intervening objectives to guide managers at all levels in their selection among alternatives.

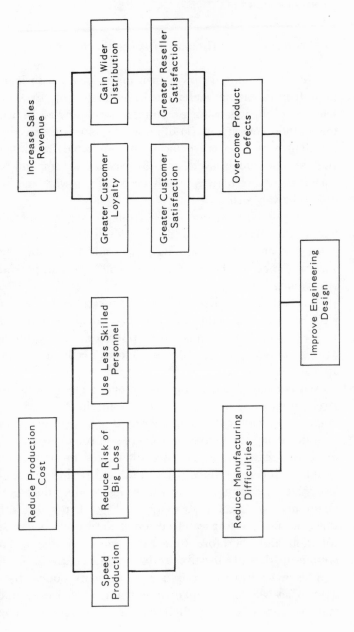

Figure 3. A hierarchy of objectives, constructed from the bottom.

(This process also helps discover objectives that have been overlooked.) Then, when they make any of the myriad decisions that arise, they will know the specific ends they are after and how those ends contribute to the attainment of higher-level goals, up to and including the firm's ultimate objectives.

Without such a developed hierarchy of objectives — explicitly stated and discussed, and preferably diagramed — there will be confusion about what standards to apply in selecting among alternatives. The result of this confusion will probably be a number of mistaken choices.

A well-developed hierarchy of objectives yields another major benefit: it qualifies each intervening goal by referring specifically to its higher-level purpose. For example, companies generally want good labor morale in order to increase productivity and reduce costs, thus enhancing profitability. If the executives know that they pursue good labor morale only to raise profits, they will pursue that goal only to the extent that it increases productivity and therefore lowers cost, and not for its own sake. And unless they realize their higher-level reason for seeking good labor morale, they might adopt costly measures that *did* improve morale but did *not* increase productivity and actually increased unit labor costs.

The process outlined here applies primarily to policy decisions and the development of detailed business strategy. However, farther down the hierarchy one comes to specific problem decisions. How these decisions are made depends on intervening goals, which vary with managers' ingenuity in perceiving special opportunities, their knowledge of the effectiveness of the means at their disposal for achieving particular ends, and the company's own special strengths and weaknesses. Thus development of a hierarchy of goals produces a custom-designed combination of intervening strategies, all directed toward achieving clearly specified ultimate objectives. By using a common hierarchy of objectives, executives and managers will make mutually consistent decisions down the line that will, ideally, contribute to the firm's overall strategy.

MILWAUKEE REVISITED

In the Milwaukee example, sales of Company A's major appliances fell for several months in succession. This fact caused deep worry for the company's Midwest regional sales manager (the person technically responsible for sales there); for his boss, the general sales manager; and for Mr. X, the independent distributor for Company A's products in the Milwaukee region. All felt committed to increase sales in Milwaukee and to achieve the firm's sales goals. They were very clear about their objectives. Each was acting as if regional sales targets were goals to be pursued for their own worth.

But high sales are only one of several goals of Company A. They are typically desired not for themselves but to facilitate the achievement of higher-order objectives, such as profit. The hierarchy chart in Figure 4 presents a simplified schematic of the goals the firm must achieve in order to have high profits.

On examining this chart, it becomes apparent that a decline in sales does not necessarily lower profits. For example, the distributor may have stopped selling to small, distant, poor credit risks and increased his profits in the process; he may have stopped selling to a few large price-cutters who were discouraging other retailers from carrying Company A's product line; or he may have discouraged some retailers from buying for a while in order for them to reduce their inventories and pay off their indebtedness. In other words, the sales decline could have reflected sound business policy rather than sales inefficiency. Indeed, efforts to increase Company A's sales in Milwaukee might have a lasting adverse effect on its position in the Milwaukee market.

Increasing the Milwaukee sales might also have detrimental effects on Company A's sales in other markets. One of the characteristics of a distributor network is the interaction among the distributors for a firm. What Company A does in Milwaukee will affect distributor attitudes in other regions. If these other distributors feel Company A has been unfair with the Milwaukee distributor, their morale may fall. As a consequence, they may turn their attention and efforts toward other manufacturers' products.

Figure 4. A hierarchy of objectives related to profitability.

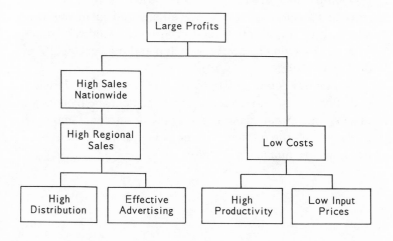

A firm rarely pursues a single objective. However, its executives often focus on instrumental goals and lose sight of other, perhaps conflicting, instrumental goals and the ultimate goals to which they are intended to lead. Consequently, they may act in ways that can have an adverse impact on their firm's performance.

SUMMARY

A favorable climate for good decisions requires the explicit and detailed statement of objectives. Certain goals are ultimate; others are intervening goals that help us achieve the ultimate ones. A firm's intervening goals are (or should be) based on an assessment of its strengths and weaknesses. Companies should try to lead from their strengths and avoid their weaknesses.

There are several levels of intervening goals in the strategy of any organization. These can be depicted in the form of a hierarchy. An effective method of constructing a hierarchy of objectives consists of (1) defining the ultimate objectives, (2) identifying alternative means of pursuing the goals at intervening levels, and (3) selecting among and balancing these alternatives. It is also possible to construct a hierarchy of objectives by starting below the very top and then asking, "Why do I want that?"

A well-developed hierarchy of objectives, explicitly stated and thoroughly understood by management, helps decision makers know what standards to apply in selecting among alternatives. Without such a statement of levels of objectives, decisions are unlikely to be effective.

3
MODELS

To decide wisely, we must understand the phenomena involved in our decisions. Decisions about matters of which we are ignorant can only work out well by lucky accident. What, then, does it mean to "understand" something? In most cases, it means to "know what it is and how it works." More specifically, understanding a phenomenon implies knowing of what elements it is composed, what each element does, and how the elements fit together.

Understanding varies widely in degree. Perhaps the lowest form of "understanding" is thinking that we know—but being wrong. This is far more likely to cause error than not knowing and recognizing that fact. The highest form of understanding is to possess a complete and valid *model* of the phenomenon. But what is a model?

MODELS DEFINED

Tersely defined, a model is a simplified replication of reality that identifies its main components and (usually) indicates how they are interrelated. The following aspects of models deserve emphasis:

1. A model is a simple version of a more complex reality; the degree of simplification varies according to the use for which the model is intended.

2. The purpose of a model is to illuminate a real-life phenomenon; some simplification is required for ease of understanding and for clarity.

3. Although simplified, the view of reality presented by a model does include its main elements and often their relationships; only the nonessentials are omitted.

4. The model depicts reality for a particular purpose and a particular audience; the best model for one individual or one purpose might not be the one that is most helpful or illuminating for another person or a different purpose.

5. A model is an intellectual tool, a device that assists in the thought process. Its value therefore is to be assessed primarily by the validity of the conclusions or decisions to which it leads.

6. A model can be expressed in a wide variety of media.

The Inescapability of Models

Everyone who thinks uses models. One will not usually reach a useful conclusion by facts alone, even though we all know people who take the position that "the facts in the case dictate the solution to my problems." People who express this view are distrustful of theories and typically begin their analysis of any problem by "gathering all available facts."

One reason that many people place a high value on facts is the history of scientific discovery, which can be viewed as a cemetery of now-defunct theories. Some trace the demise of most theories to the collection of facts that disproved the prevailing theories and suggested new ones.

Theories, then, are seen as "soft" and facts as "hard." Fine, but how do we know which facts are relevant to an issue unless we have some theory about it? Most data are ambiguous and have no meaning unless they are illuminated by a theory. Executives often possess enormous bodies of data about such things as costs, sales, labor productivity, and so forth, but do not understand the forces that determine fluctuations in costs and quality of output. As a result, they make poor decisions about those issues, even though they possess voluminous information about them.

Facts or theories alone usually will not suffice to solve real-life problems. In some situations, a fact is the crucial element in a decision. Suppose, for example, that a firm finds its packaging material becoming wet and losing its strength, with the result that much of its output is damaged in transit to customers. Some aspects of this situation are fairly obvious: the moisture must come from either inside the package or outside; also, other packaging materials might not be weakened by equal amounts of moisture. To these theoretical propositions, the decision maker must add a few facts. Factual analysis may establish that the plant environment is highly humid, thus explaining the difficulty; a change in packaging material might overcome the difficulty without increasing cost significantly.

On the other hand, suppose all we have is two facts: that the packaging material is becoming wet and thus weakened and that the plant environment is highly humid. In the absence of a theory that establishes a significant connection between these facts and identifies the possible implications, the facts are useless; for example, they may lead to a futile attempt at explaining how the high humidity in the plant arose and how this affected the structural strength of the packaging material. In other words, the facts in this hypothetical case were crucial only because we already possessed a satisfactory theory about them.

Decision makers need most what they don't possess. If they have a valid theory, they need data; if they have data, they need a valid theory. They require an understanding of the phenomenon that includes both facts and theories — in short, they need a complete model.

Effects of Deficient Models

We have already referred to models as descriptions of how things work. Most people need models in situations involving complex appliances. When an appliance ceases to operate and we "open it up," most of us are totally baffled by what we see and cannot think usefully about correcting the difficulty. Lacking even slight understanding of the appliance, we cannot possibly make valid decisions about how to repair it.

A related example involves one's first exposure to an unfamiliar phenomenon. In such a situation, one looks for a parallel in past experience. For example, when Americans observe a cricket match for the first time, they often are bewildered. Most try to find similarities to baseball — the sport they know that involves bats and balls. Given the fundamental differences between baseball and cricket, these people never do understand cricket. Thus a major obstacle to understanding results from having a misleading or inappropriate model.

People sometimes are torn between two conflicting models, as in the following incident. One of the authors visited France in December 1962, when the French currency was shifting from the "old franc" to the "new franc." The old francs were worth only one percent of the new. For a while, both old and new francs circulated side by side. On arrival at the airport, the author found himself with some shiny five-franc notes (each worth $1.00 in U. S. currency) and with some dirty copper coins that said 20 francs. The coin apparently was worth four times as much as the note, to judge by the number of francs each represented.

As he started to tip the porter who handled his baggage, the author felt strongly that something was wrong. His view (or model) of a currency system was one in which shiny notes are much more valuable than dirty coins; on the other hand, his view of the number system was one in which twenty francs are four times as valuable as five. He could not bring himself to select a coin or note to give the porter; he felt almost in a panic and started to walk first in one direction and then in another. He ended up by holding out his money to the porter and asking him to take a fair tip.

Now consider a situation in which several people are equally well informed — that is, have the same facts — but express different views about the same subject.

Four mothers are discussing what they would do about a troublesome five-year-old child in the playground if the child were theirs. One is for a rigid regimen of discipline: "Just let him step out of line, and I'd let him have it until he learned." Another prescribes more parental attention and love: "Just show him that he need not be naughty to get the attention of his mother, and he'll behave like any other five-year-old." A third takes the position that she'd "lay down the rules without emotion and administer punishments that are in line with the offense and as much as possible tied to the offense." The fourth simply states that "some children are born good, and others are difficult to handle from birth, so whatever you do won't have significant effect."

The mothers all have considerable personal experience with five-year-olds. *They prescribe very different remedies for precisely the same situation because they have different models of child behavior.*

Similarly in business, the decision makers' conscious and unconscious models largely account for the decisions they make. Conflicting opinions can often be resolved by having the disagreeing parties state their models explicitly. Sometimes one can easily infer models from the decisions made or the opinions expressed; however, that is a backward way of going about it. Besides, it is hard to do and often results in error.

It is difficult to overemphasize the need for awareness of our models and for making them explicit. Many executives are unaware of the models they are using; yet these models critically affect the decisions they make.

For example, every executive has some (generally unconscious) model of "the dynamics of human relationships." But when it comes to making a decision regarding a boss-subordinate problem, most executives will not examine their own models before making the decision. If they *did* examine their models, they might find some questionable assumptions (theories) in them — some favorite "rules of thumb" that may be wholly inappropriate in the present case. Suppose an executive's rule of thumb is that "people respond unfavorably to criticism." This executive may then fail to give valuable feedback that might keep an employee from making similar errors in the future.

In the Milwaukee example, the vice president of marketing might have the following model of sales dynamics: "If sales go down, it's because the competition is cutting prices." A decision based on that kind of model will certainly be different from a decision based on the rule of thumb that "if sales go down, it's generally because there is some problem with the distributor." A VP who realized that he held either of these models would recognize their crudity and search for other causes for a sales decline. Reliance on unconscious models can — and frequently does — lead to serious error; thus executives' awareness of and ability to state their models are vital in making good decisions.

Forms That Models Can Take

Explicit, valid models are powerful tools in decision making. Models take myriad forms and can be expressed in a wide variety of media. As a business tool, a model depicts reality for some particular purpose and for a particular audience; its value depends on the specific user and the intended purpose.

Models need not be highly refined, structured, and mathematical; anything that illuminates by simplifying and identifying key elements may be a valuable model. Additional value is added if the relationship among the elements can be described. To strive for structured mathematical models is fine, but a decision maker cannot afford to ignore other kinds; the number of useful structured mathematical models is tiny relative to the number of models that may be suitable in a given situation. The following are the types of models that most executives use.

Checklists

A checklist usually is a catalog of factors to be considered in the course of making a decision. Although it is intended primarily to guide a decision maker's behavior by identifying the items to take into account, it also conveys a crude picture of the phenomenon about which the decision is to be made. Often such a picture can be extremely illuminating, especially when one is trying to communicate information to someone who knows little about the situation. For example, a list of the main parts that make up an automobile or the human body would provide a helpful beginning toward understanding how they work.

Such a list can be even more helpful if it is a selective list (indicating only the main components) rather than an exhaustive one. And it can be still more helpful if it groups items in some relevant fashion, such as according to similarity of function. For example, it might list the key systems in an automobile (ignition, electrical, combustion, steering, braking, and so on) or in the body (nervous, gastro-intestinal, skeletal, circulatory, muscular, respiratory). A crude checklist that simply groups items according to their importance — the extent to which they influence the phenomenon in which one is interested — would also illuminate the issue.

Analogies

Very likely, most of our first models of any phenomenon take the form of an analogy — a way of explaining things by focusing on their similarities with other phenomena. Teachers are constantly driven to the use of analogies when more direct efforts to explain something unfamiliar fails.

In the field of business, one finds many useful analogies. Efforts to improve labor morale have been likened to courtship; the individual items in a product line can be considered analogous (for pricing purposes) to members of an athletic team; the behavior of firms in many markets can be said to resemble the actions of "have" and "have-not" nations in international politics.

One common analogy is the scale. Many figures of speech revolve around it: "weighing the evidence," "the decision is hanging in the balance," and so forth. If a certain weight is applied to one side of the scale, it must be offset by things on the other side or it will change the balance.

The enormous value and critical role of analogies in the learning process and in scientific discovery is only now becoming recognized. By using analogies, we come to understand what is new to us mainly by building upon what we already understand. That is, we liken the new phenomenon to another phenomenon that we understand quite well and then seek out and specify the difference between the two. In that way we arrive at our model of the new.*

Structured Models:
Organization Charts, Flow Diagrams, and Matrixes

Visual structures are often used to convey the *relationships* of various elements. In the field of business, certain of these structures are quite common. For example, the organization chart conveys the notion of "level" — indicating the superior and the subordinate, the general and the more specific — and shows groupings of departments.

Flow diagrams vary widely in their complexity but usually contain the key features of an organization chart and also show sequence and priorities. Lines varying in thickness, solidity, and so forth can be used to designate the nature of the roles played by different parties or steps in a process; the addition of arrows or colors can contribute additional dimensions and illumination. Mainly, flow diagrams are used as models of processes such as planning, production, scheduling, and communicating.

The matrix is one of the most simple, flexible, and powerful models that can be applied to business phenomena. For example, starting with the hypothesis that the behavior of firms in a certain marketplace is determined mainly by two factors, their age and their size, one could develop a matrix that would identify a number of different "types" of firms. Using the same matrix, one could distinguish the behavior of different firms, ranging from the large old firm to the young small one, with respect to, say, prices, product innovation, or expenditures on advertising.

---

* See Donald Schon's *Displacement of Concepts* (London: Tavistock Publications, Ltd., 1963) for a clear and insightful discussion of this process, with extensive illustrations from mankind's intellectual history.

Iconic, Analog, and Symbolic Models

Models replicate the real world by various devices. Iconic models, such as a scale-model globe or a photograph, closely resemble the phenomenon they are intended to replicate. They ordinarily are far smaller than reality and permit the viewer to perceive it from a new perspective. Analog models, such as thermometers, graphs, and the like, represent one phenomenon by another. Such models are usually simpler, clearer, and more easily manipulated than the reality, so they help in analyzing the effects of changes in the different variables. Symbolic models (as we define the term here) are those that employ mathematical or logical symbols. They possess the particular virtue of being amenable to mathematical manipulation, and they go well with computers.

That is of course just a partial list of models that can be used in business decisions. A model builder has a very large number of media in which to express his view of a real-world phenomenon. Some media are better suited to model building for particular phenomena than are others.

In the course of applying a model to a decision problem, the decision maker will have to make a subdecision as to *which* model to use. People tend to translate their own models into the most commonly used medium. This is convenient but not always the best path toward understanding. Often, using more than one model will help clarify the situation.

One warning: the medium used to represent a phenomenon may truly become its message in some cases. Certain types of models incorporate a "style" and a particular way of viewing the underlying phenomenon. For example, the reliance of economic theory on geometric models could not help but lead economists to stress those variables that are amenable to geometric treatment and to de-emphasize those that are not.

How Models Are Formed and Used

Decision making involves a number of high-level mental processes and abilities, such as logical deduction, memory, analysis, evaluation, imagination, and intuition. All of these can contribute to the building and use of models. When people "think"—that is, try to figure something out—they work on internal counterparts of the outside world. They develop constructs or models in their minds that they believe duplicate the phenomenon they wish to think about; they then work on (examine, manipulate) those internal models to reach conclusions that they will apply to the outside world. We could say that the decision maker's mind is simulating—working on a representation of reality rather than reality itself.

Imagine yourself as a top-level executive who received a report from several associates that one of your subordinates, a manager, was seen in a semi-intoxicated condition in the office on three separate occasions during the preceding two weeks, confirming a vague impression that you had formed in one brief meeting with him. This factory manager has had a brilliant record during his eight years with the firm and was being groomed for a top-level post. Assume that your associates asked what action you planned to take.

Your mind could perform in various ways. It could return an answer almost immediately, perhaps to the effect that the factory manager should be called in straightaway and given a firm but friendly admonition to mend his ways. Or it could build a construct with which to conduct some experiments.

In the latter case, the brain places on its workbench a representation of a man who possesses the main characteristics (say, he is proud, emotional, reasonable, and intelligent) that you believe the factory manager to possess. Your mind then tries some experiments, some of them designed to explain why such a person would suddenly start drinking to excess and others designed to explore such a person's reaction to measures that might be taken to stop his drinking.

The choice and the results of those mental experiments depend on your past experience with similar problems, "facts" about which you have read, the mental equipment you have for conducting such experiments, and so on. You will probably end up with at least one and possibly many theories about the causes of your subordinate's drinking and about how best to overcome each of them.

In exploring possible remedies, you might mentally experiment with a heart-to-heart talk, a reprimand, a threat, fatherly advice, advice to visit a psychoanalyst, or a conversation with the man's wife to see how the man on your brain's workbench would respond to each of these strategies. Clearly, you could not do all these things to the actual manager; you can only do them to your internal construct of the man.

The validity of the conclusions that you draw from such experiments will depend heavily on the accuracy of your model of the man. For example, if the "internal" factory manager responds favorably to a heart-to-heart talk but the actual factory manager does not, your approach will not produce the desired result.

Model building is not always tied to specific decisions. It goes on more or less continuously, as the mind builds on what it has already come to understand. We may begin our approach to a new phenomenon by using analogies to old phenomena; as we add to or modify the analogy, we come to understand the new phenomenon in its own right, and as we gain increased experience with the phenomenon, we make our model increasingly detailed.* Eventually we may develop a model that is almost as complex as reality.

---

* For a most interesting and clear discussion of this process and the controversy that surrounds it, see Mary B. Hesse, *Models and Analogues in Science* (Notre Dame, Ind.: University of Notre Dame Press, 1966).

Many explicit models do exist for application to specific problems. Decision makers whose understanding of a problem is sketchy might be well advised to apply a standard model in an attempt to clarify the issue. Such a model will teach them things they didn't know about the phenomena they need to understand.

Let's assume we confront a complex problem about which we are not very well informed. We have available – in a book or a report – something that purports to be a model of the phenomenon around which the problem revolves. Perhaps it is a matrix or a flow diagram. In any event, the model is expressed in a medium that is readily intelligible, or at least it presents no major barriers that we must overcome. How would we use the model?

First, we would probably try to internalize the model – to make it part of our own intellectual property. That means we would try to visualize the interplay of the elements depicted in the model. We can apply it to similar past situations and see how it fits. One important task would be to try to understand why the elements in the model were represented in a particular way. For example, why is one element considered prior in time to another? Why would we expect the elements to be independent of one another or interdependent? What kinds of things have been omitted from the model that we had considered important?

In the process of internalizing the model, we presumably are seeing the phenomenon in a new light. Usually the model will be only a foundation on which we can build, however. We build on the model by adding variables to take account of special features in the situation and to replicate our decision situation more accurately. We can then simulate with the help of the model; that is, we can change the value of one key ingredient and see how the model would forecast the effects of this change.

Thus the use or application of a model is a highly active process. The model user cannot simply act as a sponge and absorb what is there. Rather, the model will usually demand special efforts on the individual's part to break out of a habitual way of thinking about a phenomenon.

What Makes a Model Useful?

As we have suggested, models vary in their suitability for different individuals and different situations. The amount of help a decision maker will derive from an explicit model varies not only with the quality of the model but with its suitability for that person as well.

A model helps the decision maker if it (1) indicates elements that had been theretofore overlooked, (2) indicates relationships the decision maker had not recognized before, or (3) helps the person eliminate elements and discard relationships that were mistaken. To do all these things, it must reflect the reality reasonably well; it must incorporate the key elements and identify the main relationships operating.

But it must do more than this. A model must be in a form that is readily intelligible to the user. Some of the greatest poetry is understandable to relatively few people who have great sensitivity to language and to obscure literary references; such poetry makes little contribution to the lives of the majority of people.

Similarly, models that can be understood and applied only by an elite corps of technicians will not enlighten the vast majority of decision-making executives. The majority, then, must either use other models or employ the services of consultants who are experts in model building. These consultants will in turn be most helpful to the decision maker if they begin with simpler formulations and work their way up to the more complicated, technical ones. Only in this way can the decision maker hope to internalize the model and to apply fully his/her own expertise to the problem.

Since a model that illuminates the situation for one person may not do so for another, the evaluation of models is highly subjective. But in assessing the usefulness of a model, there are several questions that are applicable to most situations:

- Can the model be understood and applied without lengthy preparation and practice?
- Can it incorporate many additional variables, if desired?
- Does it permit introduction of dynamic elements — that is, elements that change over time?
- Does it permit easy incorporation of interdependencies among some of the variables?
- Does it permit visualization?

Once the model has actually been used, the decision maker should ask some further questions: Has it enabled me to identify opportunities or sources of difficulty and to forecast the results of outside events (or my own actions) as well as other models I have been using? If I were to continue to employ this model, would it provide greater illumination than other models? In short, one judges a model as he would any other tool: Does it get the job done? How does it compare with other tools that I might use?

Another way of evaluating models would be to use several of them — if time and resources permit — and compare their effectiveness. In applying different models, an executive will usually learn something from the very differences among them; a comparison of the variables they include and the relationships they posit will often shed new light on the problem.

MODELING IN THE MILWAUKEE PROBLEM

Sometimes a person who knows little about the phenomenon in question but does know something about models can work with an executive who is involved in the situation to produce useful models. Here we offer an example of how this process might take place in the Milwaukee situation. The vice president is conducting a dialog with a specialist in model building.

VP   *Well, as you know, our goal is to produce a model that will help us to explain and correct our poor sales record in Milwaukee — and in other cities when they arise.*

MB   Okay then, let's get started. Our first model is likely to take a fairly general form, at least at the start. By virtue of its generality, it may have quite broad applicability.

VP   *I think I understand what you said, but what troubles me is that when you speak of general models, I constantly come back to the fact that the course of a difficulty and the remedy for it usually are anything but general. An executive must know the specific details involved in that situation and deal with them in concrete and detailed terms.*

MB   Yes, I know that; however, we work our way up gradually to a highly detailed and specific view of the situation we're trying to understand. We will be wise to start by developing a broad and general model that sets down the main forces that influence sales and then, in steps, make that model more complex and specific until it incorporates all that you know and believe about the forces that determine whether sales come up to expectations.

VP   *That helps.*

MB   Good. As a start, I'd suggest that we try to explain a disappointing level of sales rather than to explain the actual level of sales that occurs.

VP   *I'd opt for doing what is easiest. Could our model be constructed to explain below-expected sales? We might then explain such sales by a below-expected level of* total *demand or below-expected levels of advertising — or more-than-expected numbers of competitors.*

MB You're very much on target. Let's do it that way at the start at least. We'll deal with far fewer factors if we explain why sales are below expectations than if we try to explain the absolute level of sales.

VP *How about the factors that I mentioned a moment ago? I'd explain sales that were lower than expected if we actually did* less *to move the merchandise than we expected to do or if our competitors did* more *to push their sales than we expected.*

MB That's very reasonable; in a minute, I'll ask you to list the things you may have done less of or that competitors may have done more of than was expected. Now, I want to ask you a difficult question: What other problem or process does this question of explaining sales below expectations remind you of? That is, is there anything that is analogous to it, in your opinion?

VP *That* is *a tough question; frankly, I'm not sure that I even understand it.*

MB Let me try again. As you spoke, I thought of a parallel to the problem that we're discussing. I see a scale; on one side are the things your firm does to promote sales and on the other are the things your competitors do. Now, you expected your firm and your rivals to put particular amounts of sales effort on the scale and therefore expected some particular balance on the scale. If unexpected things went on one side of the scale, they could be offset by things on the other side or could change the balance. That is a model to explain the relationship between actual and expected sales. Now, can you think of any analogy like that which conveys your picture of why sales fall below expectations?

VP *Yes, I can see how to do that. As the notion of the scale conveys, the level of sales that our firm achieves reflects offsetting efforts on the part of our competitors and ourselves — plus possible changes in the environment that may affect most of us equally. Frankly, I'm hard pressed to find a better way of visualizing that phenomenon than the scale. Does your experience suggest any other analogies?*

MB   Let me see. How would this analogy do: I'd compare your sales experience in a market to the position that your son attains in his class. His class standing will reflect his efforts in class and in doing homework, his native ability, and the efforts and abilities of other students in the class.

VP   *That's interesting and a little more illuminating than the scale analogy. But shouldn't we move on to more specific ideas about what might explain why sales were below expectations?*

MB   Good idea. Let's now set down the most simple, but universally applicable, model. It may be called a dependent-independent variable model. We start with the phenomenon we want to explain — in this case, sales below expectations. We call this the dependent variable. Then we list the things on which it depends. Those we call the independent variables; some people would call them "causes."

VP   *I see what you're doing. This approach should be applicable to almost any phenomenon you're likely to meet because it's wholly free from content. Whereas the scale notion implies some of the processes at work, this dependent-independent variable model just helps to organize your thinking.*

MB   What we need, of course, is an understanding of what will help you with your particular problem of sales below expectations in Milwaukee. To meet that need, we must know many specific things about your particular situation. What would be true for appliances would not be true for detergents or liquor sales. The more our model incorporates the forces that operate in your markets, the better it should help you understand and solve your problem.

VP   *I can see that. Shouldn't we move along and try to identify the factors that might cause sales to fall below expectations for a major appliance in a market like Milwaukee? Is that your message?*

MB   Yes, it is. Now, what are the most important factors that operate in such markets to influence your sales performance with major appliances, measured against sales targets?

VP *Okay. If you asked me why sales in a market sometimes fall below expectations — where our expectations were realistic to start with — I'd have to mention the following kinds of causes. First, our competitors were cutting prices. By that I mean that either the distributors carrying competitive lines or some of their major retail outlets were charging substantially less than our people were charging. Usually, I might mention, if that were to happen, our people would fairly quickly learn of it and take countermeasures. But that's not always the case.*

MB That's very helpful. Just for the record, I'd want to treat separately the cutting of prices by retailers and by distributors.

VP *That's all right with me. Another reason for disappointing sales has been some notable success by a competitor. He may have developed a superior product feature or have stumbled onto an effective national advertising campaign. A few years ago, one major competitor got his hands on a strong national TV program and hurt us in most markets. And, whenever a competitor adds a new feature that we don't yet have, we suffer in sales for a while.*

MB Remember that we're trying to explain why sales were unexpectedly low in particular markets; that would seem to confine our interest to factors that are not national in scope. But go ahead; you're doing just fine.

VP *In a local market, if our distributor or retailers were to let up on their efforts to push our products, we'd show poor sales results. A strike, or a closing down of a key retail account, would show up in diminished sales. Or, if our distributor were to deliver sets that weren't carefully inspected before being shipped, we'd possibly have lots of customer complaints that would hurt sales. I don't know whether you want me to go on; I could list many additional ways in which our distributor and retailer might hurt us.*

MB At this point, maybe you should only suggest some other factors that might make sales disappointing, though we may come back to the failings of retailers and distributors again before we're finished.

VP   *Then let's shift to this business of advertising, which means to be a fairly potent influence on appliance sales. If our competitors were to increase their advertising substantially, we'd be hurt. Or, if our retailers and distributors were to cut down on their advertising, I'd expect our sales to fall. Of course, the quality of advertising is also important.*

MB   What I've gotten thus far is that such factors as price (at retail or to retailers), weight and content of advertising, the various things that retailers and distributors might do to satisfy or dissatisfy customers, their service activities and the like, are the main factors that influence sales. I don't want you to list everything you could possibly think of, because our model must be selective. We want an accurate but simplified picture. Of course, to produce such a picture, you generally must create a more complex picture and then drop out some things as being relatively unimportant.

VP   *Could you set down a model that would incorporate what I've said already so I can see what a dependent-independent variable model would look like?*

MB   Sure, that's easy. The ratio of your actual level of sales to your expected level of sales is a function of relative price, relative weight of advertising, relative impact of advertising appeals, relative support of retailers, relative sales efforts of your own distributor, relative attractiveness of product features, relative appeal of product design, and so on.

VP   *I can see the logic and value of that kind of model. Why don't we settle for it?*

MB   We could probably do a lot worse, but how can we tell whether we have developed a really good model until we have examined several of them? Often, one stands out far above the rest.

VP   *I'd be interested in any other "standard" types of models you can tell me about.*

MB   I have only a few standard approaches that are likely to fit most situations. For example, one can usually model a situation as an input-output system. As I define it, such a system consists of elements that combine to perform some particular function, with each part having a special mission. A complex machine, like a car, has many subsystems: the electrical system, the braking system, the combustion system, and so forth. Each system takes something in and, after it "does its thing," puts something out.

VP   *An automobile takes in gasoline, oil, and water and produces transportation, I guess you'd say.*

MB   Right. Let's see what happens when we attempt to explain a disappointing level of sales as an input-output system. Would you like to give it a try?

VP   *I'll see what I can do with it. The input of the system includes such things as our sales efforts and those of our rivals and the demands of customers, let's say; the output consists of our sales and competitors' sales. The system itself takes these sales efforts and consumers' demands and turns them into customers' responses—actions of purchase or non-purchase.*

MB   That's a good answer as a start. But the key question to raise is whether that view of the matter is useful. Does it help you understand why sales fell below expectations and possibly suggest what you should do about the problem you face in Milwaukee?

VP   *I'd not be able to answer that offhand. It isn't clear to me just what is working on the inputs to produce the outputs. What would be our "system" in this case? Would it be firms in this industry? The "market"—whatever that means?*

MB   That's a good question. I'd expect the answer to depend on what you believe turns the inputs into outputs; it might be a combination of things including the manufacturers, the retailers, distributors, customers, et cetera, and maybe even more than these. If that were the case, our system would have many elements, each of them fairly complicated.

VP   *But that's what we should expect. After all, our dependent-independent variable model did refer to distributors, retailers, customers, and what we and our competitors do. If that's the case, presumably our input-output system should include those elements. Isn't that so?*

MB   Yes, I'd think so. Not all models would include precisely the same ingredients, but one would expect them to include the same *key* ingredients.

VP   *Do you know any other standard models you can tell me about?*

MB   Let me see, we've talked about looking for analogies, the dependent-independent variable approach, and the input-output system. The last I can suggest is the "noun" method.

VP   *That certainly sounds odd. What do you mean by a noun method?*

MB   It goes this way: you characterize the phenomenon you're trying to model by a noun. In this case, we're talking about disappointment, frustration of goals, failure to achieve one's objectives. These words or phrases describe the failure to achieve one's sales goals.

VP   *Okay, I can see how these nouns describe our Milwaukee situation, but how does that help me develop a model?*

MB   In several ways. First, as we string out these nouns, we find that they clarify the essence of the phenomenon. That is, this method directs your attention to the heart of the matter. In this case, for example, it is that you had goals or expectations that were not realized. The nouns also convey the impression that your failure is due to your own shortcomings or the strengths of your rivals.

VP   *I'm not sure that I got all that from these nouns, but go on. In what other ways do you benefit from this stringing out of words?*

MB   What it gets you to do is search for the key mechanism or processes that are involved in the phenomenon that you're trying to illuminate with a model. What's more, you do it with one or a few words that carry lots of associations and connotations that are suggestive, at the least, and often will direct your attention to key aspects of the phenomenon that might otherwise be overlooked.

VP *I'd like to change the subject, if I may. We've been talking about how to produce models, but you've alluded to the fact that a number of widely used models already exist right now. Wouldn't one of them meet our needs in this case?*

MB I doubt it. I've referred to models developed and used mainly by "management scientists" and operations researchers. Those models are amenable to mathematical expression and to at least an approximate mathematical solution.

VP *That would certainly seem to be an advantage.*

MB Not necessarily. When you don't understand a phenomenon well enough to express the relationships among the variables in mathematical form, you just can't have a useful mathematical model. In many cases — even with business problems — we are in that situation where we can't express the relationships between the determining factors and the dependent variable with which we're concerned in quantitative terms. Take our problem of the failure to achieve our sales goals in Milwaukee. Could we state the relationship between weight of advertising, relative price, appeal of advertising messages, and actual sales relative to expected sales in quantitative terms?

VP *No, we've tried to do that sort of thing — or at least our market research department has — many times, but without success. Oh, I see now. That means we're merely left with our old friend, the dependent-independent variable model. It identifies the factors that determine the extent of our sales achievement, without stating them in numerical terms. If we could quantify those relationships, then possibly we could explain why sales were disappointing.*

MB   That's true, but we probably wouldn't need a mathematical model for that purpose. If we knew, for example, that the Milwaukee distributor was making less effort to sell your product or that your advertising appeals were ineffective, we would have an answer, without any mathematical statement being necessary.

VP   *That's a good point. Our diagnosis of the trouble needs only an indication of the factors we should examine. Maybe we would need a mathematical model if we wished to predict the result of actions we might take — like increasing our advertising.*

MB   For certain kinds of action, such a model would help — assuming that we could develop a valid model of that kind. However, what we would need more than anything else would be some bright ideas about how to motivate our distributor, or some clever ideas for a better advertising campaign. We need good ideas more than we need formulas for making forecasts. And if we're dealing with bright ideas, almost by definition we are dealing with something whose effects cannot be forecast accurately.

VP   *This discussion certainly has been an eye-opener for me. First, I see that nonmathematical models serve our needs, or at least the most important ones, most of the time. Second, I realize that we can't have valid mathematical models for most of the problems that I'm concerned with — like sales, personnel, advertising, distribution, product design, and so forth. I'm getting the impression that as a business executive I mainly need models that will help me understand such things as human nature, people's prejudices, associations, aspirations, and fears.*

This dialog gives an indication of the process of building nonmathematical models that take into account such factors as causes or "working causes" (in this case, suspected causes that have operated in the past), and suggests that several different models be tried and evaluated according to their usefulness in the given situation. The dialog could be carried further in order to develop two or three models to the point where a plan of action or a remedy might be suggested.

Of course, one does not usually find pairs of executives and model builders working together in business to produce models like these. But the process can be used by, say, an executive who is coaching a subordinate who in turn is dealing with a problem first hand, on the scene. The executive, who may not know all the details himself since he has delegated that responsibility to the subordinate, can nevertheless help the subordinate make sure all relevant factors are taken into account and their patterns of interaction examined.

The main factors that might be involved in a business decision situation such as the Milwaukee example might include uncontrollable ones, such as the general economic, industrial, and regional environments, and more controllable ones, such as financial and human resources. These factors can be listed or diagramed, but if they are merely listed, it is wise to indicate at least which ones are interdependent. The important thing is to be as specific as possible in the construction of the model. Only if you delineate a model carefully can you avoid the decision pitfall of "Oh, I didn't think of that."

SUMMARY

"Understanding" means having valid models. Composed of facts and theories, models take a wide variety of forms and can be expressed in many different media. They can be unconscious pictures based on past experiences or they can be complicated mathematical constructs.

Most of the models decision makers use are highly personal to the individual. Usually they embody analogies to those phenomena with which the decision maker is familiar. Models are generally built in stages by transferring knowledge from a familiar subject to one that is unfamiliar and then altering and refining the transferred material. Besides simple analogies, the other kinds of models commonly used by decision makers include checklists, organization charts, matrixes, flow diagrams, and iconic, analog, and symbolic models.

Models underlie virtually every decision. Two decision makers will often come to different conclusions because they are using different models. It is important to be explicit in identifying the models one is using. Explicitness helps decision makers improve their own models and communicate information about a problem to others.

The kinds of models that are helpful to business executives vary widely with individual taste, experience, and the intended application. A truly useful model helps decision makers identify elements they had overlooked, indicates relationships that were unrecognized before, shows which elements or relationships were mistaken, *and* is readily intelligible. Decision makers also must put effort into internalizing the model in order to break out of their habitual way of thinking about a phenomenon. In short, using a model is a highly active process.

4
SIGNALING SYSTEMS

In producing decisions as a manufacturer would produce a product on an assembly line, decision makers must know when to "turn on the machines." They must make *timely* and *appropriate* decisions to seize opportunities that had been overlooked or meet dangers that went unnoticed.

Let us return to our Milwaukee situation as an example. The following is a dialog between the vice president in charge of marketing (VP) and the market research director of the firm (MRD).

VP *We'd better have a talk about Milwaukee. Am I right in thinking that last quarter's sales are off by 25 percent?*

MRD Yes—and the preceding quarter's sales were down 10 percent.

VP *I know. When I got that earlier report I called Joe Davis, the Milwaukee sales manager, and he told me that some big orders had been delayed and that this quarter would compensate.*

MRD Where did he get that story from?

VP *He got it from our main distributor out there.*

MRD   That's funny. I had to call that distributor about some questions on commissions, and he told me that the local competition was price-cutting us to death.

VP   *Maybe both answers are right — or maybe neither. But what's wrong with our information system? Why weren't we on top of this before we lost so much ground?*

MRD   We had our hands full last quarter with Seattle and Atlanta. We didn't have time to think about a 10 percent decline in Milwaukee.

VP   *We shouldn't have to think about it. Joe Davis should have handled it — and maybe he would have if he, and we, had known that the original 10 percent drop wasn't just a matter of some delayed orders.*

MRD   Well, you can't have complete breakdowns of everything. We'd drown in the paper.

VP   *Surely we could have some system of reporting so that we would get detailed information only when it was needed. Our main job shouldn't be to put out specific fires. We ought to be creating better procedures for our fire departments.*

This dialog illustrates the wrong way of becoming aware of problems. All of us have experienced this phenomenon; our society seems unable to recognize the existence of certain problems until they have reached ferociously destructive levels. Our environment must be virtually destroyed before society recognizes the existence of a serious ecological problem; drug addiction must reach epidemic proportions before it receives attention; large cities must be wracked with riots before our serious urban problems are treated on a national level; and so on in a dismally endless list.

Business enterprises cannot afford to follow society's way of becoming aware of problems. Yet executives, particularly those in large organizations, often find that they have discovered the existence of a problem only after it has reached the crisis stage. Similarly, opportunities may slip away because they were not grasped at the right time.

The more complex the organization, the greater the likeli-hood that *implicit* problem-detection methods will not be adequate. The corner grocer with two clerks is directly involved with all aspects of his business, from customer relations through inventory and pricing problems to labor problems. Chances are that he will notice most of his problems early. The typical executive in a large business organization, however, is separated from his problems by layers of people and must deal with a broad range of matters that need attention. How, then, is he to know that a problem has just arisen that requires a decision on his part? How can he know that an opportunity is at hand that he should seize? These matters should no more be left to chance or to ad hoc methods than should the questions of switching to a different product on a multiproduct line.

Each executive needs an explicit system that will call attention to decision situations as they arise in the various areas under his/her control. We call such a system a "signaling system"; it is a kind of early-warning system designed to alert the executive in time to make a needed decision. A good signaling system consists of two elements: a *reporting system* and a *signal level*.

Many executives do have some sort of reporting system. Quantitative reports detail the current situation hourly, daily, weekly, or on some other regular basis. Sales reports, absenteeism records, financial audits, shelf life reports, and market share reports are among the many missives that crowd the manager's desk. Usually there are also unscheduled or ad hoc reports such as those on management information systems and on organizational effectiveness.

Combined with these reports are a variety of informal methods such as direct personal observation, discussions with subordinates, suggestion boxes, and comparing notes with other executives in similar situations. Naturally, such systems are valuable; managers who use them skillfully often savor the fruits of success. However, there are two potential deficiencies inherent in such detection systems.

First, they can seriously overload the executive. As a manager steps up the hierarchical ladder, the volume of reports that must be audited usually increases, often to the point where it can become almost physically impossible for that manager to find the time both to detect all the problems or opportunities in the areas of major responsibility and to attempt to deal with them. The overwhelming majority of the information reported is of no particular interest to decision makers; and worse, the large amount of irrelevant information makes it very difficult for them to locate the useful bits.

The second deficiency, paradoxically, has to do with *too little* information. Any single reporting system highlights certain symptoms and tends to miss others completely. For instance, the usual company reporting system will call attention to sales declines, increases in unit costs, increases in inventory, and similar kinds of problems. But it will not pick up equally important problems of lost sales, losses of goodwill, too-low prices, and so on.

Such systems detect problems mainly because certain types of information are readily available and not because the problem is important. For instance, it is easy to measure proportion of defectives and very hard to measure product quality, so there is likely to be a reporting system based on the former but not one based on the latter. And it is generally far easier to measure direct costs than it is to measure opportunity costs (that is, the costs of missing an opportunity), so there are many kinds of reporting systems based on direct costs but almost none based on opportunity costs.

Generating more reporting systems to deal with more

areas of interest might seem to be one way to counteract this deficiency, but it might exacerbate the other deficiency: demands on the executive's time. The typical harried executive could be forgiven a few caustic comments if someone suggested that he ought to add more reporting systems to those that already keep him fully occupied.

What harried executives need is something more than just reporting systems. They need reporting systems plus signal levels. A proper combination of the two will lessen their burdens rather than add to them, even if the number of reporting systems is increased. The kind of signaling system we are going to discuss here is based on the idea that *only* the relevant information is reported to the executive. And what we mean by "relevant" is that kind of information which strongly suggests that something is not going as it is supposed to go.

The executive's main job is to make decisions about things that deviate from the "normal." Once a policy decision is made, it can be left alone until some signal indicates that a new kind of decision must be made. In our Milwaukee example, the vice president of marketing and the market research director did not need to be told that sales in, say, Atlanta were on target. They did need to be told that sales in Milwaukee were slumping badly. If sales in Milwaukee had, on the other hand, suddenly surged to unprecedented highs, the executives would also want a signal that some action might need to be taken — if only to discover what the sales force was "doing right" so that it might be carried over to another division.

In short, if something is as it is expected to be, then the executive should not spend time on it. This is the principle that underlies the technique called "management by exception."

The simplest illustration of a signal level can be found in the "two-bin inventory system." A company's stock of widgets is kept in two bins. Whenever widgets are needed, they are taken from the first bin, and when that bin is empty, it is time to reorder. Meanwhile widgets are taken from the second bin. The signal level is an empty bin.

The term "two-bin system" is also used to describe any kind of inventory system in which a predetermined order size is fixed for each item and a given order is made whenever the stock on hand drops to or below that amount. Suppose there were 10,000 items on such a system and that the stock levels were reviewed once a week. Clearly, there would be no reason to report the actual stock levels of each of the 10,000 items each week. The only information that needs to be reported is the list of items for which the stock level has dropped to the assigned level and which therefore require ordering.

Of course, the described two-bin system is too simplistic an analogy for most types of managerial decisions. In such a system the action to be taken as a result of the signal is automatic and always the same. This is definitely not the case for more general signaling systems, which will be discussed in the next chapter.

Constructing a Reporting System

As we have indicated, a signaling system consists of two parts: *a reporting system* and suitable *signal levels.* The development of the reporting system can in turn be conveniently divided into three steps: (1) the identification of the disorder or opportunity to be detected; (2) the description of the symptoms of the disorder or opportunity; and (3) the selection of an indicator to provide the signal. We will discuss these three steps in order and then proceed to the determination of signal levels.

We have already noted that all too often the only aberrations detected are those for which relevant measures happen to be reported. To avoid such happenstance, one must begin by defining the unusual occurrences that should be detected. This is easier to do for problems than for opportunities since it would be impossible to design a system that would catch all opportunities that are off the beaten track. Yet some of the following steps can be applied to opportunity signaling systems also.

First, it is necessary to have a model in mind, preferably explicit, before one can hope to identify the problems. Once you state the characteristics of a healthy operation, you can say that disorders represent departures from these characteristics.

Suppose you conclude that a disorder is anything that adversely affects the worth of the firm to the stockholders, or anything that adversely affects production efficiency, or anything that causes insufficient production on the afternoon shift on May 22, or anything that infuriates workman X on the morning shift.

Clearly, this progresses from the too-general to the too-specific. Either extreme is bad. The too-general cannot be translated into operational terms. What, for example, is the effect of a sharp change in the proportions of total sales of two products on the worth of the firm to the stockholders? On the other hand, the too-specific would cause a breakdown in the whole managerial system. The production manager cannot concern himself with the morale of each individual on his production line, even if suitable reporting systems were available.

There are two principles involved in achieving the right level of generality. First, you should formulate the model in terms of the functions that are under your control. This helps avoid excessive generality. Thus the sales manager should have an explicit model of a good sales situation and not necessarily one of a smoothly running company.

In avoiding the other extreme, excessive specificity, the

crucial concept is economic importance. Why is the production manager not directly concerned about the exact state of the morale of workman X on the morning shift? Simply because the economic consequences of the morale of workman X are not likely to be significant enough to justify a production manager's attention. (If the economic consequences were, or might be, sufficiently severe — for example, if X were the shift union stewart — the production manager then would undoubtedly be directly involved.)

How can you determine whether the disorder is of sufficient economic importance to the operation to justify your attention? The discussion of signal levels, in this chapter, and of agenda decisions, in Chapter 5, will help answer this question.

The second requirement in the construction of a reporting system is the description of the symptoms of an aberration — good or bad. Aberrations, or disorders, can range from explicitly quantitative to entirely qualitative. Some of the quantitative disorders result from restrictions imposed on the operations by top policy decisions. For example, if a sales manager has been told to achieve a certain product mix, then this product mix will surely have been included in his/her model of a good operation. Similarly, if an advertising manager has been given the objective of reaching at least 60 percent of a particular socioeconomic class with the advertising message, then this will be included in this person's model of a good operation. For such quantitative statements the symptoms of a disorder are obviously directly definable in quantitative terms.

Unfortunately, however, the majority of possible disorders are likely to be qualitative ones. For these the description of the symptoms is not so easy, but nonetheless possible. A "disorder" that would never produce any observable symptoms is not a meaningful disorder.

The most common difficulty in selecting a symptom in a qualitative situation is that sometimes no symptom seems to capture the real essence of the disorder. For example, a production manager will probably identify bad morale among the workers as one potential problem. What are the symptoms of this? Excessive labor turnover, excessive absenteeism, excessive time spent not working, low productivity, poor-quality work, work stoppages — these are some of them (unfortunately, they appear too late). Yet no one of them seems to capture what most people mean when they speak of bad morale.

The reason for this is probably that each of us thinks we know introspectively what it would mean if we ourselves had bad morale; since these subjective ideas differ, each of us is likely to feel dissatisfied with any list of symptoms for such a disorder. Unfortunately, this is one problem we simply have to live with. Since we cannot get inside other people's heads, we often have to attempt to reason from their actions.

Another common difficulty is that several disorders can produce the same symptom. One example is the symptom of insufficient sales. This could be a symptom of customer dissatisfaction with product quality, too high a price, poor distribution, low salesmen's morale, poor advertising, and many other disorders. We must avoid a possible misunderstanding here. The explicit models held by sales managers, at least, will ordinarily include some requirement on sales. Therefore, insufficient sales is *itself* a potential disorder, not just a symptom. Still, if the sales manager wants to find the *underlying* disorder, he or she will treat insufficient sales as a symptom.

After the symptoms of the various potential disorders have been described, there remains one more requirement for the reporting system: the selection of indicators of the potential disorder. This requires finding suitable quantitative measures of the *symptoms*. The ease with which this can be done depends on the nature of the symptoms. In many cases it is perfectly straightforward, but in other cases it may be very difficult.

The easy end of the spectrum of possibilities comprises cases where there is one major symptom of the disorder and where it is obvious how to express it quantitatively. For example, insufficient sales is a disorder whose symptom is simply sales, which are already quantitative. This applies equally to total sales, product sales, regional sales, sales by type of outlet, and so forth. The same kind of simplicity exists in the measurement of the quality of the production line output by the number or proportion of defectives. For cases such as these the indicator for the potential disorder is obvious. Most of the common reporting systems have this type of index.

An intermediate case arises when there are several symptoms for the potential disorder but each of the symptoms is easily measurable. Let's look at the potential disorder of poor worker morale. Earlier we listed some of the symptoms of this disorder: labor turnover, absenteeism, low productivity, poor work quality, and so forth. Most of these symptoms are fairly easy to measure; however, some of them — for example, work quality and time spent not working when supposedly on the job — are not.

In such instances the question arises whether to attempt to measure all the symptoms or to be content with those symptoms that are easily measurable. This question really deals with the worth of information and must be answered using the arguments we will develop in the next chapter on agenda decisions. As we will see there, it is not particularly difficult to get an adequate answer to the question.

Suppose it is decided to use turnover, absenteeism, and productivity as sufficient measures of worker morale. Then another question arises: Should the three separate measurements be amalgamated into one index number of worker morale by a suitable mathematical formula? Historically, the major reason for so doing has been to avoid overburdening the executive with reports. But since the use of signaling systems eliminates a great deal of this burden, there may not be sufficient reason for an amalgamated index number. Valuable information could be lost when such amalgamation of measurements occurs. It is easy to think of situations where the executive would be anxious to know, for example, that absenteeism had increased sharply but without changes in the other two measurements.

More difficult cases are those for which there is one major symptom but it is not at all clear how it can be measured. Take the potential disorder of customer dissatisfaction with product quality. An obvious symptom, and one that is immediately measurable, is the number of overt customer complaints. But is it a symptom for the particular disorder we are considering? Complaints are more nearly indicative of the number of defective units sold than they are a symptom of a general mild discontent with performance. For this disorder it might be necessary to define the symptom directly in terms of some procedure for questioning the users of the product—such as prepaid post cards attached to the product, questionnaires mailed to the users, or interviews. This, of course, incurs some cost and possibly even requires the aid of a market researcher.

The most difficult case is one where there are various symptoms of the potential disorder but many of them are not measurable and no one of them seems to be particularly satisfactory. As an example, consider an item that is of very great importance to deans: the quality of the faculty. In constructing an explicit model the dean will undoubtedly identify one specific potential disorder as "insufficient research, in the sense of contributions to knowledge." What are the symptoms of this? Too much time spent in consulting or on vacation?

But many professors are seminal thinkers and yet carry heavy loads of consulting. Too few publications? Do textbooks count—are they contributions to knowledge or simply compilations of existing knowledge? And what about publications in obscure periodicals for which the author cannot even give away the reprints? Is it perhaps really a question of the opinion of professors at other institutions? But often, surprisingly, such opinions are primarily hearsay and are many years behind the times. And so the listing of possible symptoms can continue, each one being dubious as an index of the potential disorder.

Note that the real difficulty here is *not* that the various symptoms cannot be measured. For example, publications can be counted and an attempt can even be made to measure the importance of each publication by using the "citation index," which shows how often a given article has been cited by other articles. The real difficulty is that one has the distinct feeling that no combination of these measurements is an adequate measure of faculty research. To make an analogy, a report that gave accurate measurements on each feature of a woman's face would have missed the essence of the issue if it neglected to say whether she was good-looking or not.

This analogy suggests how one can proceed when all else fails. A jury of experts can be formed to make estimates of the characteristic in question—faculty quality in our example, beauty in the analogy. A conventional scale can be used, say from 1 to 10. Reliable measurements can be obtained in this manner. It is almost always better to have explicit measurements based on experts' judgment than to have no measurements at all.*

Although the jury system is a possible last recourse for ob-

---

* This is exactly the system that was used in several major attempts to evaluate graduate schools. See, for example, Allan M. Cartter, *An Assessment of Quality in Graduate Education* (Washington, D.C.: American Council on Education, 1966).

taining measurements, it is worth noting that experts often find remarkably devious ways of measuring things that seem to laymen to be very difficult to measure. One book that is particularly full of striking examples of clever measurement systems is Eugene Webb, Donald Campbell, Richard Schwartz, and Lee Sechrist's *Unobtrusive Measures: Nonreactive Research in the Social Sciences.** The methods discussed range from using dirtiness of pages to measure the differing degrees of readership of various sections of an encyclopedia to counts of empty liquor bottles in trash to determine patterns of liquor sales.

With these kinds of examples in mind it would be pleasant to be able to suggest that probably some kind of devious measurement could be devised for almost any symptom. Unfortunately, we think that the reality is otherwise. Most of the clever measurement procedures for sociological phenomena depend on the fact that the people whose behavior is measured are not aware of the procedure.

Suppose (as an absurdly oversimplified example) that an office manager decides to measure the work level in her office by weighing the waste paper each night. When the office personnel becomes aware of this measurement device—as they inevitably would—they will probably respond by adding ample amounts of heavy trash to the waste paper so that the office manager will find a gratifying upward trend in work level. This example is not very realistic, but it calls attention to a major and remarkably widespread problem in measurement: the *index number fallacy.*

This fallacy must surely be one of the manager's most common blunders. It occurs whenever someone takes the measurement of the symptom to be equivalent to the original disorder. Stated so boldly, it might appear that only a very

* Chicago: Rand McNally & Co., 1966.

unthinking person could commit such an error. No reasonably intelligent executive, for example, would assume that because absenteeism is unchanged, morale is likewise, or that because one candidate for a position had better marks in school, that person is necessarily the better prospect. Yet somehow, in the workings of the organization, the index number fallacy is likely to be committed. How can this happen?

Here is an example: an advertising manager, in developing his model of an effective campaign, has included some statements about the impression the advertising has made on potential or actual customers. When he comes to define the symptoms of a disorder in this area (namely, that the advertising has made an insufficient impression), he will discover that it is very difficult to measure exactly what he has in mind but that there are various measurements that might be taken as indexes: (1) readership data showing the number of people who read the magazines in which the advertising was placed; (2) "noting scores" showing the proportion of people who actually noticed and remembered the advertisement; (3) brand registration data showing the proportion of people who noticed the ad and associated it with the brand name; (4) claim-conviction data showing the proportion of people who were convinced by the claims made for the brand; and (5) intent-to-buy data showing the proportion of people who intended to purchase the brand as a result of the advertisement.

It is clear that the progression within this list is toward measurements more closely in correspondence with the advertising manager's definition of effective advertising. However, it is also true that measurements further down this list are somewhat more nebulous, generally more variable, and always more costly. Therefore, the advertising manager will have to do some careful thinking before he selects an index number. Suppose he chooses noting scores, a frequently used measure of magazine advertising effectiveness. The stage is now set for the organization to commit the index number fallacy.

Since noting scores are being used to evaluate advertising effectiveness, it follows that the people who create the advertising are being evaluated by noting scores. These people, then, can be expected to aim for high noting scores so that their efforts will be suitably rewarded. In effect they say: "If the boss wants noting scores, we'll give him noting scores!"

Unfortunately, there are a variety of ways of achieving noting scores *without* having effective advertising; for example, once upon a time a picture of a pretty girl in a bikini would have gained high noting scores for male readers. The index number has been taken as the goal rather than as a tool for avoiding the underlying disorder. The result is that the index is maintained at high levels while the disorder can run rampant.

The moral is clear. Noting scores may be a valid index of advertising effectiveness *if* everyone concerned is trying to achieve effective advertising, but *not* if the people creating the advertising are trying to achieve high noting scores. The same kind of conclusion holds whenever the index number fallacy could occur. There is no surefire way to avoid this fallacy, but the first line of defense is for the executive to be aware that it can occur. This, together with a judicious occasional use of other indexes, is probably sufficient to avoid the most pernicious effects of this fallacy.

Now that we have explored the vagaries of reporting systems, let us turn to the other ingredient of signaling systems.

SETTING SIGNAL LEVELS

If you have persevered through the steps discussed in the preceding section, each of the index numbers you have selected will be included in a reporting system. Each of the reports will be "disorder-oriented" in the sense that it is based on one or more indexes that have been specifically selected as indicators of potential aberrations (bad or good). But in most cases the indexes will show that there is no potential disorder, and you need not waste time on such reports. You need to be promptly informed *only* when some area of your responsibility is not going as it should and hence may need your attention. This need is met by an appropriate signal level for each index.

We mentioned earlier that the basic idea of a signaling system is typified by a two-bin inventory system. In such a system, when the inventory of an item falls to a predetermined level, this is a signal that an order is needed. We want to construct the same kind of system for each of the index numbers you have selected. This requires the determination of a specific value of the index number such that whenever the actual index number reaches this value, you will be so informed. This specific value is the signal level. (Sometimes there are two signal levels for an index number; in this way both problems and opportunities can be detected.) You need not be concerned with the index number unless it reaches the signal level.

The establishment of signal levels follows procedures that are well known in statistical quality control. Although the application of such procedures to the construction of signaling systems will probably require the assistance of a statistician, only a few elementary notions of probability theory are needed to follow the basic argument involved.

The design of the signal level requires a preliminary step: the selection of a target level for the given index number. This is primarily the executive's task. The target level of the index number is that value which the executive accepts as being a satisfactory or acceptable level for the given index.

Sometimes — as for sales volume — this will mean that the executive does not want the index to be too much lower than the target level. Sometimes — as for absentee rate — it will mean that the executive does not want the index to be too much higher than the target level. And sometimes — as in the case of clerical salaries — he/she will not want the index to diverge too much in either direction from the target level.

There are a variety of methods for determining a target level. The target level could be some assigned standard, such as a budget figure predetermined by higher policy. Or it could be based on historical levels achieved. Or it could be a theoretical maximum for the index in question; this is particularly useful when there is no historical information on the index number.

Another alternative is to establish target levels on a comparative basis for similar units. (This is sometimes called the use of the deadly parallel. For example, one sales region can be compared with a similar region, in the sense that neither should fall too far below the other.) Further, target levels can be based on reported data for comparable businesses. This is commonly used to establish target levels for salaries for clerical personnel. Finally, when all else fails, the executive can establish target levels on an intuitive basis — what he/she thinks the index ought to be.

It is most important that the target level should be realistic. There is some risk of being unrealistic in each of the above methods, but the risk is most acute when intuitive target levels are established. If a young newlywed were to demand a target level of zero spats for an index number of marital bliss, she or he would be very likely to be quickly and repeatedly disappointed. And this would not necessarily be a sign of an unsatisfactory marriage.

One of the authors has seen a striking example in the business world where unrealistic target levels were set for hiring junior and middle management. The targets were achieved, with the result that the company had a truly extraordinary group of highly competent young employees. Unfortunately, there was neither sufficient challenge nor sufficient possibility of advancement to satisfy such outstanding young people. The result was that they soon sought greener pastures elsewhere. This company would have been in a far better position if it had set target levels for hiring that were more consonant with the quality of the positions available.

Once the target level has been established, the signal level can be determined. If the index reaches the selected signal level, the decision maker will be informed that the situation may require his or her attention.

To arrive at a precise signal level, you must perform a balancing act. You want to be informed as soon as the system has changed from its basic state to indicate that something is "deviant" in the form of either a problem or an opportunity. But you do not want to take action unnecessarily. Two types of error, then, are possible: failing to take action when it should be taken and taking action when it is not necessary.

Naturally, since both these errors are potentially costly, you would like to make the probabilities of these two types as small as possible. However, as the probability of one is decreased, the probability of the other usually increases. To arrive at as precise a signal level as possible, the executive must estimate the costs of each type of error and balance them. Examples of this balancing are offered in Appendix A. (For reasons described more fully in Appendix A, increasing the number of observations in the distribution curve will decrease the possibility of both kinds of error simultaneously; however, increasing the number of observations has of course a cost too.)

Estimating a signal level is best done by a statistician, although it can be (and is) also done at various less sophisticated levels. Every decision maker has some kind of signaling system, implicit or explicit, and the two kinds of error exist for every system. To develop the most useful signaling system, it is necessary to make the cost judgments as precise and explicit as possible.

Summary

In order to know when problems or opportunities arise that require decisions, the decision maker needs a signaling system. An effective signaling system consists of two elements: a reporting system and a signal level.

Most executives have some sort of reporting system, composed of quantitative reports and informal methods of fact finding. But in most organizations, there are two potential drawbacks inherent in the reporting systems. First, they can seriously overload the executive by providing a large amount of irrelevant information; second, they can provide too little of the right kind of information. The kinds of problems or opportunities that such systems detect tend to become more a function of what is easy to report than of the importance of the issue.

The construction of a good reporting system can be divided into three parts: identification of the aberration (good or bad), description of the symptoms of the disorder, and selection of an indicator (index number) for the disorder. When the disorder is of a qualitative rather than quantitative nature, describing a symptom can be difficult; likewise, when it is not clear how a symptom can be measured, obtaining a quantitative measure is difficult. One way to obtain a measurement of a symptom is to form a jury of experts to rank the elusive quality on a scale. No matter what the method of measurement, however, it is important to avoid the "index number fallacy" — taking the measurement of the symptom to be equivalent to the disorder itself.

In addition to a reporting system, a signaling system requires a signal level. The determination of a signal level requires a preliminary step: selection of a target level (the value the executive accepts as being a satisfactory or acceptable level. At the signal level, the index deviates enough from the target level to warrant attention.

In creating the signal level, one makes use of the concepts of random variables, standard deviations, and normal distributions. There are two kinds of error inherent in this procedure — taking remedial action when it is not necessary and failing to take action when it should be taken. The costs of these two potential errors must be balanced carefully.

5

The AGENDA DECISION

In the previous chapter, the vice president of marketing and the market research director decided that there really was a problem in Milwaukee. Now they must decide what, if anything, should be done about it. This is the agenda decision—a key step in the decision production process. The following dialog illustrates some of the dynamics involved in this step.

VP *You're not seriously proposing that I waste my time on a regional sales problem, are you? I'm so busy now that I don't know whether I'm coming or going.*

MRD Well, I would certainly agree with you if it is in fact a "waste." But what makes you think it is?

VP *I've got a perfectly good sales manager for that territory. It's his problem.*

MRD The fact that the sales are still down would suggest that he hasn't found a way to handle it. Aren't you supposed to backstop your junior executive?

VP   *Yes, but I know that Joe Davis is good. He thinks the distributor isn't doing his job. Since he hasn't figured out what to do, we probably can't either. After all, if our distributor isn't up to snuff, what can anyone do? We'll probably just have to change the distributor.*

MRD   But that will cost $40,000. I thought you said you didn't intend to "waste" your time. What about wasting money?

VP   *Well, if I have Bob put three or four days on that problem he still won't find any other solution. Then it will cost $40,000 plus his three or four days. That's the waste.*

MDR   Your whole argument assumes that there is nothing to do but change the distributor.

VP   *I hear that this fellow in Milwaukee has suffered a change in character. Suppose we do find the reason. I'm no psychoanalyst, so I won't be able to do anything about it. And I'm not about to wait three years while he gets straightened out by a headshrinker.*

MRD   It might be cheaper if you did. And there may be other solutions possible. You know very well that it may not be the distributor at all. There's a good chance it's price cutting.

VP   *Suppose it is. We'll probably just have to live with it there like everywhere else. I'm not going to find a new way to deal with price cutting.*

MRD   You'll never be sure if you don't put some time on the problem.

VP   *We've already wasted too much time on this problem! We have more important things to do. Don't you know we have a strike in our Peoria plant? The whole year's sales picture is being affected by that strike. I feel I have to stay on top of that situation. Too much is involved there. The settlement may cost us an arm and a leg.*

MRD   So you'll spend two weeks on it, and it will cost an arm and a leg plus your two weeks. I think I've heard that argument fairly recently.

VP   *You're using debating tricks. The two situations are totally different.*

MRD   Oh, come on; you know they're quite comparable. It's true there is a difference in the total amounts involved in Peoria and Milwaukee, but there is enough involved in Milwaukee to justify putting a man on it for a few days. Is Bob so busy you can't spare him?

VP   *Maybe you're right. I'll see if I can put him on it for a while. Let him find out the real cause of what's happening out there.*

The two executives in their dialog have quite rightly emphasized questions of "waste" and costs. And they have reached an agreement of sorts. But they have not taken explicit account of all the relevant costs, and they have not considered the probabilities of the different outcomes of their possible courses of action. We want to find a more adequate means of analysis than the unstructured approach taken by these executives. Let us begin by discussing the general structure of this kind of decision and why we call it an agenda decision.

AFTER THE SIGNAL IS RECEIVED

A signal level has been reached and the executive has been informed. What should be done? First, we need to be clear as to what the executive knows and does not know as a result of the signal. Two points need emphasis. First, there may not be any real problem or any real opportunity that requires action. Any signaling system has some probability of producing a signal simply as a result of random variations when the underlying process is functioning perfectly normally. Second, the signal at best shows that a potential decision situation exists. It does not tell anything about the cause of the situation or what should be done to remedy it or take advantage of it. This, then, is the position of the executive when receiving a signal: there may not really be a "disorder," and if there is one, the executive does not know specifically what has happened or what might best be done about the situation. Now what?

The answer to this question requires an agenda decision on the part of the executive. The fact that a subject is placed on the agenda means that the potential importance of the subject justifies some use of the executive's time. Since the executive's time is limited, the inclusion of any item on his agenda means that other items cannot be included. If the executive decides to place the potential disorder on the agenda, it will be necessary to determine how much time and what resources to devote to it.

At this point, it is useful to distinguish between two major kinds of decisions. Specific action or inaction (ignoring the situation) will be called the *terminal decision.* In our Milwaukee example, the terminal decision might be to replace the distributor, fire the regional sales manager, add another sales person, lower prices, or do anything else intended to resolve the problem.

But before the terminal decision is made, the decision maker might decide to do any of a large number of things that are intended to provide additional information so that a better terminal decision can be reached. We will call a decision of this kind an *information decision.* In the Milwaukee example, information decisions would include making a statistical analysis of past Milwaukee sales, calling the regional sales manager in for a conference, sending an assistant to Milwaukee to investigate the situation, and so forth.

Sometimes (but by no means always) there is a whole series of information decisions, each being made as a result of analyzing a previous decision and each representing a greater commitment of resources to a potential problem or opportunity. An actual example will illustrate this.

An oil company was considering the possibility of using a linear programming formulation in order to determine the optimal storage and distribution plan for a major geographical area. The company decided to make a feasibility study to determine whether linear programming could be used for this and at what cost and with what benefits. The feasibility study was made by six consultants who were specialists in the use of linear programming in similar situations. As a result of the feasibility study, which took about nine months, the linear programming formulation was subsequently undertaken.

Clearly, the feasibility study was the result of an information decision. The study indicated that thirty person-years would be required to achieve the desired formulation but that the potential benefits were more than enough to justify this. The terminal decision was to attempt to achieve the linear programming formulation of the overall storage and distribution network. But note that it had to be decided that it was worthwhile to make the feasibility study. To do this, some company personnel made a preliminary study that took a few person-weeks. Before that, one executive did a few days of research into the subject.

THE COMPONENTS OF THE AGENDA DECISION

When a signal is received, the executive must decide what to do with it — whether to ignore it, to postpone consideration of it, to have a study made to get further information, or to make a terminal decision immediately. These possibilities form part of the agenda decision.

Of course, the fact that the executive is trying to decide whether to include the problem on the agenda means that it is already receiving some attention from the executive and thus, in a sense, is already on the agenda. But this preliminary consideration may be thought of as a "once-over-lightly treatment" and is based on a quick appraisal of the alternative demands on the executive's time, the importance of the problem area in terms of the company's objectives, and so forth. If the executive is doubtful about the proper conclusion after such a quick appraisal, there is reason to put the problem on the agenda.

The executive then has many options in terms of timing. First, the problem can be given immediate priority over all other demands on the executive's attention. This would be the executive's response to an emergency situation with large possible effects on company objectives. Second, the problem might be put on the agenda as the next one in the queue of problems demanding attention. This would be the response if the executive's quick appraisal is that this problem is comparable in importance to those already in the queue. Third, the problem might be left for consideration when the executive has some idle time. Since this risks a long delay, it would not be done unless the problem is of distinctly lesser importance than others on the agenda. Fourth, the problem might be put on the agenda at some specified date in the future. This avoids the possible indefinite delay of the third alternative and yet recognizes that the problem is of lesser importance than others currently on the agenda. Fifth, the executive may note the signal and decide not to place the problem on the agenda unless the signal is repeated in the future. Thus the executive will not respond to a false signal.

There are other possibilities in addition to these. The point is that the executive has a great deal of flexibility in the timing of the agenda decision.

Executives rarely make a terminal decision without devoting some time to the problem. The second question, then, is how much attention should be devoted to the signal. Executives should think in terms of a chain of agenda decisions analogous to the chain of information decisions in our previous example.

Suppose that, on the basis of quick appraisal, the executive decides that the signal deserves some immediate attention. Then the first step might be a once-over-lightly treatment. This consists of using whatever models or information are already at hand to determine how much effort to devote to the potential problem or opportunity. A common conclusion as a result of this is that some more information is needed. The information decision might be to have some readily available data pulled from the files and to review the situation briefly with others. At the other extreme, the executive may decide to make a lengthy cost/benefit analysis.

Somewhere in this continuum of possibilities an important option arises: the executive can assign someone else the task of dealing with the problem or of getting information that will be used in the executive's own analysis. That is, after determining whether a decision is needed, when it should be made, and how much time should be spent on it, the third component of the agenda decision is *who* should give attention to the relevant signals.

It is useful here to continue our analogy of the executive as a production manager for decisions. The executive has a shop for decision production that contains people and equipment—the resources at the disposal of the executive. This shop is like a machine job-shop, and the scheduling problem is very similar to that of the factory. The executive must assign the right jobs to the right people, taking into account what they might otherwise be doing and taking advantage of each person's special skills for handling particular kinds of problems.

The fourth, and last, component involved in an agenda decision is the *depth of treatment* of a potential problem. This question must be addressed even when part or all of the problem is assigned to someone else. The amount of expenditure of effort will depend on the executive's assessment of the costs and benefits. Often the subordinate must be told how much effort is to be expended.

Suppose that in our Milwaukee example the vice president of marketing asks for a statistical analysis of past sales in Milwaukee. The statistician has no way of knowing whether he ought to spend two hours, two days, or two weeks on the project since this depends on the vice president's estimates of the potential benefits. In his assignment the vice president must therefore specify the depth to which he expects the analysis to be carried.

Most subordinates want to do the very best they can. Yet it is very rarely the case that the potential benefits from a decision justify the "best possible" analysis. The subordinate's tendency, then, is often to do too good a job. This can be prevented if the executive specifies the depth of the analysis.

These components of the agenda decision—whether (and when) an aberration should be dealt with, how much time should be devoted to it, who should attend to it, and what the depth of treatment should be—have been discussed in terms of the positive things the executive wants to achieve in making the agenda decision. A different point of view is also worth considering. This might be called the negative approach: what are the things the executive wants to *avoid* in making the agenda decisions?

Three Kinds of Waste

Stated negatively, the objective of the agenda decision is to avoid waste. Waste is a nontechnical term that means, roughly, avoidable costs.

The first kind of waste is that of foregone opportunities;

its cost is usually calculated by estimating the profits that might have resulted had some other course of action been chosen.* Opportunity costs are involved in problem decisions as well as in opportunity decisions, because resources spent to solve problems will than be unavailable to pursue opportunities.

The second kind of waste can be described thus: effort that does not create change is wasted effort.

The argument that justifies this statement is simple. Let us compare two hypothetical situations: in the first a decision is made to market a new product without any further studies; in the second a decision is made to market after the expenditure of time and money on one or more preliminary studies. In either case, the worth of the marketing decision is the same, but in the second case only, there has been an expenditure. In short, the effort has resulted in a cost without any corresponding benefit. It must be carefully noted that this argument does not depend in any way whatsoever on the correctness of the decision that would have been made without further effort.

The third kind of waste that we want to single out is the waste that occurs when the results of the analysis suggest a change in the course of action but there are circumstances that prevent the decision maker from following the indicated changed course of action. This kind of waste is similar to the second kind in that the effort produced nothing of value.

There are two main reasons why an indicated course of action cannot be adopted. First, the decision maker may not have control over the necessary variables. Suppose an advertising manager decides that he could select more effective advertising media if he had better identification of his product's potential customers. He therefore commissions a market

---

* Many executives would want to incorporate a risk factor in such calculations.

study to accomplish this purpose. The market study demonstrates that the high-potential users of the product are the set of families with some precisely defined socioeconomic characteristics. Suppose, for the sake of argument, that 1 percent of the total of families are of this type. The advertising manager now hopes to utilize this information in the selection of media; his goal, of course, is to select those media that reach a higher proportion of the given family type. But the media inform him that they cannot effectively reach this family type. At this point the advertising manager is in the situation we have described. He could choose more appropriate media on the basis of his market study — except that the lack of certain vital information prevents him from doing this. The positive contribution of the study is therefore zero.

The second major reason why an indicated course of action may be impossible to follow is that there may be legal restrictions, company policies, or self-imposed constraints that stand in its way. For example, a study that discovers a better packaging material for a product may be without value if the material is likely to run afoul of citizens concerned about environmental pollution so that its use is prohibited by company policy.

In the context of the three major kinds of waste, we might look again at the dialog about the Milwaukee problem at the beginning of this chapter. The two executives are talking about waste throughout much of their discussion. The vice president begins by saying that he can't waste his time on the problem because he is too busy. This, of course, depends on the opportunity costs. Then he says that any effort will be a waste because it will only confirm what the regional sales manager has already concluded — that the distributor is not doing a good job and must be changed. This would be an example of our second kind of waste, the expenditure of effort that does not lead to a change in the course of action. Then the vice president goes on to claim that even if a reason is found for the distributor's "change in character," he will not be able to do anything about it. This would be an example of the third kind of waste: the results of the expenditure cannot be translated into concrete action. Finally, the decision to assign a subordinate to the problem ought to depend on the alternative assignments that could be given to him; this is another example of the first kind of waste.

The two executives, then, are attempting to deal with the agenda decision in terms of the kinds of waste we have discussed. However, they are doing so in a somewhat haphazard way. It is quite unlikely that the best decision will be reached with such an approach. What is needed is an explicit analytical procedure that can be used for such decisions.

THE DECISION TREE

A most helpful tool in the agenda decision is the decision tree, a generalized structure for organizing the key elements in the decision problem. This model can be thought of as a kind of road map showing the various routes that can lead from the current situation through a series of choices and occurrences to a final outcome.

A completed decision tree has three components: (1) the skeleton of the tree, which pictorially represents the possible courses of action, the outcome, and the relevant states of the world (sets of variables over which the decision maker has no control); (2) the probabilities of the various outcomes and states of the world; and (3) the payoffs (or costs) associated with the outcomes.

The skeleton of the tree is a set of nodes joined by straight-line segments. In our presentation the top node represents the decision maker's situation now, and there will be a straight line leading from this node to each of the other nodes, which are alternative courses of action available immediately.

Consider the decisions involved in a single bet as an illustration. Suppose you are offered a bet on a coin toss. If the coin shows heads, you will win $10; if it shows tails, you will lose $5. If it is an honest coin, this is clearly a desirable bet. But let us construct the decision tree for this little decision problem anyway. You have two courses of action: bet or no bet. Therefore, there will be two nodes below the "now" node, connected to it by straight lines; this is shown in Figure 5(a).

The skeleton of the tree is continued until the decision problem is completely resolved. The "no bet" node certainly terminates the decision problem, so there is no straight line leading from this node. But if you bet, then the coin will be tossed, with two possible results: heads or tails. Therefore, we need two lines leading from the "bet" node; each of these terminates the decision problem, so the skeleton of this decision tree is complete. The result is shown in Figure 5(b).

A decision tree is completed by adding payoffs and relevant probabilities to the skeleton. A payoff must be entered under each terminal node. The change in assets that results from a branch leading to a terminal node is always a correct measure of the payoff—unless there is a question of the measurement of utility. If you do not bet, then there is no change in assets. If heads occurs, then your assets increase by $10. If tails occurs, then your assets decrease by $5. This gives us the tree in Figure 5(c).

Before we evaluate these alternatives, we add the relevant probabilities. We must distinguish between nodes that represent courses of action and nodes that represent outcomes (or states of the world). Nodes that represent courses of action are under the decision maker's control—he or she can select the one that looks best. The nodes that represent outcomes affect what happens to the decision maker, but the decision

Figure 5. Construction of a decision tree for a simple bet.

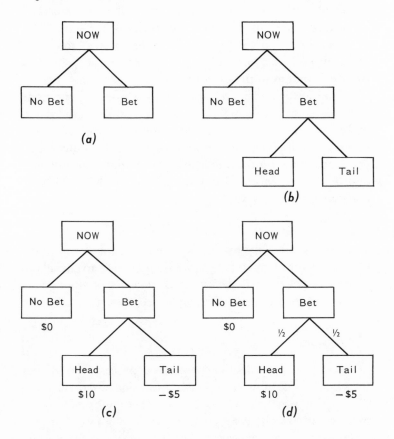

maker has no control over them. Thus, in our example, we have two courses of action — bet and no bet — and we can select whichever of these we prefer, but we obviously cannot select whether the coin will show heads or tails, so these are outcomes.

The rule for adding probabilities to the decision tree is simple: the probability of each outcome must be written beside the line leading to that outcome. In our example, the probability of heads and the probability of tails are each $\frac{1}{2}$. Therefore, the completed decision tree is as in Figure 5(d).

After the tree is completed, it must be analyzed to place a value on each decision point. This is easy to do. We work from the bottom to the top of the tree.

If the lower nodes are outcomes, the worth of the node immediately above them is the weighted average of the values of the outcomes, or what is called "expected value." It is computed by multiplying the value of each possible outcome by the probabilities on the line leading to the outcome and adding the results. In our decision tree the worth of the "bet" node comes out this way:

$$\tfrac{1}{2}(\$10) + \tfrac{1}{2}(-\$5) = \$2.50$$

This means that "bet" has an expected value of $2.50. In the long run, over many such bets, we would expect to gain about $2.50 per bet. (For a decision tree analysis of the agenda decision of the Milwaukee example, see Appendix C.)

SUMMARY

A key step in the decision production process — taken after the signal has been received — is to determine how to deal with the decision problem. The decision maker might make a terminal decision right away — that is, decide to ignore the signal or to take some specific action — or make one or a series of information decisions aimed at refining the model of the situation.

Essentially, the agenda decision consists of four components: whether to take action; how to take the action (including what priority the problem shall have on the agenda); who should give attention to the signals; and what depth of treatment the decision problem should receive. The executive can make the agenda decision on the basis of the positive things that can be achieved or on the basis of avoiding waste (avoidable costs). There are three basic kinds of waste: opportunity costs, effort that does not create change, and effort that suggests change which cannot be carried out.

To avoid making the agenda decision in a haphazard manner, one can use a decision tree, which organizes the key elements in the decision problem and points to the best course of action. The decision tree consists of (1) the skeleton of the tree, which shows the possible courses of action, outcomes, and relevant states of the world (variables over which the decision maker has no control); (2) the probabilities of the various outcomes and states of the world; and (3) the payoffs associated with the outcomes.

6
The QUEST for CAUSES

As we indicated in the previous chapter, one output of the agenda decision process might be a resolution to get more information. If we are dealing with an opportunity decision, we want to search out the kernel of the good idea—to find out what we did right or what is so good about a new proposal—and see whether there is anything in that kernel that can be applied to other areas. If we are dealing with a problem decision, we want to find the cause of our difficulties. Since problems are easier to explain in the context of a production line of decisions, this chapter will emphasize problems rather than opportunities.

No foolproof method exists for finding the causes for real-life problems; those who seek the cause of difficulties must expect to fail frequently. They should also be alert to situations where it would be more prudent not to make the search at all. Of course, we do not need a total understanding of all causal relationships that exist in our enterprise in order to solve our problems. We need to know just enough about the sources of troubles, and sometimes "just enough" is simply the "remedy point"—one factor we might change and thereby eliminate the problem.

Why Detection of Causes Is Difficult

In explaining why something is what it is or why some event happened, we usually face a choice: we can explain why the situation changed from what it was just before, or we can explain its nature "from the ground up." Let us consider the second, more complex, alternative first.

Take a very simple and all-too-familiar example of an employee (Mr. Jones) who has turned to drink and no longer performs his duties well. What factors could explain such a "happening"?

Assume that we have exhaustive and reliable information about Mr. Jones. Specifically, we know that he has come to believe that he will never achieve his lifelong ambition of holding an executive post and has been depressed by that realization. In his depression, he sought escape and relief in drink.

To track down the cause of his heavy drinking further, we might first ask why he concluded that he would not become an executive. The answer, we will assume, is that his supervisor said some harsh words to him one day when he was guilty of an oversight. (The supervisor was in a very ugly mood at the time and really did not mean what she said.) Contemporaneously, we might assume, Mr. Jones had been having a running battle at home with his oldest son, who was bidding for increased independence by challenging his father's general competence. Finally, in other societies Mr. Jones might have no desire to become an executive (indeed, he might even have had no supervisor); accordingly, the general values of our culture can be considered one cause of his drinking.

The fact that Mr. Jones's desire to become an executive seemed in danger of frustration would not in itself explain his drinking. He could have reacted in quite another way, say, by working harder or by seeking another position where he might have a greater opportunity to advance into the executive ranks. Thus, many influences must enter into an explanation of his excessive drinking; all can be considered causes. In the absence of any one of them, his drinking to excess might not have occurred. (Observe, parenthetically, that without removing any of these influences, one might still cure Mr. Jones's drinking by, say, prescribing a drug or helping him cultivate some new outside interest.)

Anyone who has studied psychology knows that a particular individual's behavior is virtually unpredictable. An enormous number of influences impinge on a person even in a short period, and we cannot usually predict when the person will be in a responsive or vulnerable condition. As has been so wisely said, people are more complicated than anybody and more unpredictable than anything.

What is true of people holds to a lesser degree for most phenomena. Things happen the way they do because of the cultural, political, economic, and physical environment in which they occur, and each of these environments has many facets that bear directly or indirectly—and often mysteriously—on the phenomenon.

However, executives rarely must explain a phenomenon from the ground up; their interest usually is in why it changed for the worse (or for the better). In our illustration, an executive need not know why Mr. Jones drinks excessively but why he took to drink when and to the extent that he actually did.

Suppose Mr. Jones had been having debates with his adolescent son for some time, without drinking heavily. One might therefore conclude that the unusually harsh words of his supervisor were "the cause" of his drinking. One could easily suppose that, in the absence of those words by the supervisor—or the mood that explains them, or the factors that produced the mood—the man would not have taken to drink. On the other hand, one could just as easily suppose that had his son not given him such a rough time, he could have taken his supervisor's tough treatment without "breaking down." In fact, he may have been talked to harshly by the supervisor before.

Thus the identification of causes does not become simple —though it is simplified—by seeking the cause of a *change* rather than of a state of affairs. Changes in some factor often are associated with changes in another; however, often only under certain circumstances will the particular observed result come to pass. To explain what happened, one must take account of these surrounding circumstances. But they are most difficult to uncover because they usually do not represent any sharp break with the past; by virtue of having continued for some time, they are likely to pass unrecognized.

Must One Identify Causes of Difficulties to Correct Them?

If we confront a business difficulty, we must make three subdecisions with respect to causes. First, we must decide whether to search for the source of the difficulty at all. Second, if we decide that the first step is necessary, we must determine how much effort to devote to the search. Third, we must decide how to look for the cause.

The first subdecision makes many executives uncomfortable. It is "natural" to assume that if something is wrong, one should find the cause and eliminate it. Many people apparently share the conviction that a failure to search out causes is unscientific, illogical, and possibly immoral. After all, "nothing happens without a reason." This position leads to the conclusion that almost every occurrence has a single and ascertainable cause. That, unfortunately, is just not so. *The plain fact is that businesspeople usually cannot find the causes of their most vexing difficulties.*

There are two extreme classes of executive troubles: (1) problems whose cause is almost obvious or is readily determinable; and (2) problems whose cause cannot be found no matter what one does.

To illustrate the second case with an example from the medical profession, there are many illnesses that cause pain and death, but efforts to learn the cause have proved futile. With such human disorders, doctors can only try to relieve the pain and make the patient comfortable; a concerted search for causes would be cruel and extravagant. Similarly, executives should assume that they cannot establish the cause of certain difficulties. But how can one overcome difficulties without knowing for sure why they came about?

First, a difficulty may correct itself—that is, it may be corrected without any effort on the part of the decision maker. Second, some causes, although not self-correcting, nevertheless disappear just as mysteriously as they arose. Third, an executive can accept the continued existence of the difficulty and decide to *offset* rather than correct it. A doctor might find that a person's pancreas provides insufficient bile products and even feel that he knows the source of the trouble—and still not try to correct the source. Instead, he may simply prescribe a medicine that will provide the body with the material not produced in sufficient quantity by the pancreas. In business, an employer may recognize that employees' morale is poor because of large amounts of involuntary overtime work. The overtime work may be continued but a particularly well-liked supervisor transferred from another division to work with the employees to "offset" their poor morale.

Admittedly, one would usually *like* to know the cause of a

difficulty, for frequently it can be easily removed once it is found. We are only arguing that in many cases it is *not necessary* to know the cause in order to cope with a problem.

A fourth method of attacking difficulties for which one does not know the cause is to "start over." For example, if we have trouble with a machine and cannot locate the problem, we can just replace the machine. A worker or executive who does not perform well can be transferred or replaced.

Of course, many situations are not suited to this type of treatment. And we often "start over" and end up just where we were initially because we really did not start over. For example, it may have been the raw lubricant used on the machine that gave rise to the difficulty. Even with the new machine, the same trouble would reappear.

Many causes for business difficulties can be described by an analogy: they resemble a tree that has fallen across a path and blocked our way. Even if we knew how the tree got there, we probably would just look for a path around it. If the cause was not known, all the more reason to just accept the situation and seek some way to offset it. There would be no point in spending time trying to find out why the tree fell. Thus, although the question of whether to search for a cause is an important one in business life, it is quite possible that the executive will decide, for good reasons, *not* to make the search.

A MODEL OF CAUSAL RELATIONSHIPS

The following model should illuminate the essential nature of causes, whether we are dealing with a problem or an opportunity. This model contains the following elements:

1. The environment in which the phenomenon occurs.
2. The factors that affect the phenomenon directly. (We rarely know *all* the factors that affect the phenomenon and the extent to which they affect it.)

3. The nature of the phenomenon itself—those inherent characteristics that explain why it is the way it is.
4. The consequences of the phenomenon.

Figure 6. **A model of causal relationships.**

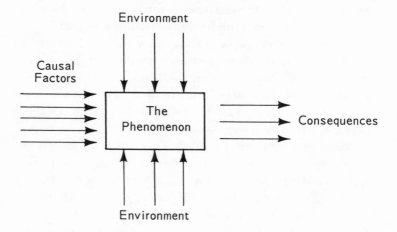

Figure 6 sets down these elements in a simple visual
model. Observe that many arrows coming from the left impinge on the phenomenon—that is, cause it. The phenomenon itself has its own "nature" that determines its responses to
those external factors. These responses, or consequences, are
symbolized by the arrows leaving the box. The entire process
occurs in an environment that affects the outcome; changes in
the environment would presumably alter the impact of the
causal factors and change their consequences. (Of course, this
means that environmental factors are, in a sense, "causal" too.
We will discuss this question a little later.)

In the context of such a model, we might say that five
major factors explain the level of sales (or morale, or costs, or

whatever). Each of these "causal factors" will typically prove to be a phenomenon that can itself be described by the same kind of model that is depicted in Figure 6. This situation is illustrated in Figure 7, which presents a highly simplified "causal net" for a decline in a firm's sales in some market. It shows several possible causes for the decline, most of which are themselves the results of several causes; each of these are, in turn, affected by a separate set of influences.

Figure 7. Causal net for a sales decline.

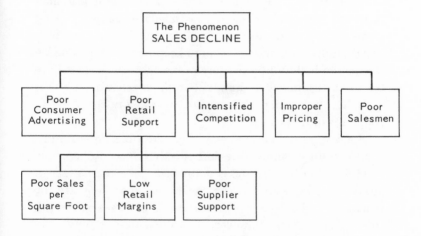

WHAT DO WE MEAN BY "FINDING THE CAUSE"?

As already indicated, we can never be certain that we have found the cause of anything—although we may be able to rule out some suspected causes. This depressing conclusion results from the possible existence of unknown factors; no method guarantees that we have considered *all* potential suspects. Must we then continue to endure our difficulty since we cannot be certain of its cause?

Not at all. Even though we cannot be certain that we have

found the cause of our difficulty in any specific instance, we may nevertheless have found a "working cause"—a factor that behaves as if it were the true cause of the difficulty. By altering that factor, we might alter the phenomenon with which we are troubled, in the way we expected.

Here is an illustration: a person's watch started to misbehave badly; it gained about a half hour every three hours. He had a hunch, based on something that his watchmaker had told him years earlier, that a particle of dust had settled on a sensitive part of the mechanism. He had no idea of what that mechanism might be or how the dust would cause it to malfunction. Anyway, he banged his watch hard against the palm of his hand several times in the hope of dislodging the dust, and thereupon the watch began to keep perfect time. Can we say that he had found the cause of his difficulty? It may have been not dust but something else in the mechanism that was remedied by sudden shocks. But we can say that he had found a working cause.

Some working causes may not be correctible. For example, if an executive cannot function effectively because her only child is seriously ill or she is depressed about the danger of atomic war, then even if she conjectures that these are the true causes, she rarely can test those hypotheses or remove those causes. Often, however, she can change circumstances (remove another assumed cause) and observe the result. If the result is favorable, she can assume that she has found the working cause.

One may ask how we can find the "real cause" as distinct from a working cause. The answer is that we cannot. Since some factor of which we are unaware may be producing our difficulty, we can achieve a high degree of certainty that we have found the true cause only by conducting controlled experiments designed carefully to rule out all errors in interpretation. Even then, we can never be certain that we have ruled out all possibilities.

To sum up, then, if all the evidence points to a particular cause for a difficulty, we can only consider it a very likely cause or the most likely suspect. Only by acting to eliminate it can we determine whether we have found a working cause. Even then, if the action taken to eliminate it is misguided, we may indeed have found the cause but failed to confirm it because of a faulty remedy.

Since it is so easy to go astray in a quest for causes, decision makers must be skeptical and cautious in reaching conclusions about causes. They must hesitate to undertake a major effort to find a working cause; or, having found what seems to be "the" cause, they must ponder deeply before they incur heavy costs in an effort to eliminate it, since they may not have found the real cause.

A Scheme for Deciding Whether to Search for "The Cause"

Decision makers who are deciding whether and how to seek the cause of a difficulty have three main alternatives: (1) to make a major effort to find the cause; (2) to make a modest effort; and (3) to make no effort at all to find the cause — either because they assume that they cannot discover the cause or because they already feel they know it. Each of these courses of action leads to subsequent outcomes and actions that are best described with the help of a diagram such as Figure 7.

If executives try to locate the cause of a problem, they will usually incur a cost, and several outcomes may result from the quest: they may uncover the cause and be able to "verify" it; they may uncover what looks like the cause but not be certain;

they may not feel any closer to knowing the cause after making the effort than when they began; or they may uncover what they mistakenly believe to be the cause.

But we have gone only part of the way; the outcome of our search for causes is important only if it affects the firm's actions thereafter. That is, we search for causes in order to learn what action to take to eliminate them. Even if we find a verifiable cause of our trouble, we are not helped much if we cannot take effective action. (This represents the third type of waste discussed in Chapter 5.) Even worse, we may try to eliminate a cause and end up by making conditions worse. Some types of elective surgery illustrate this possibility: patients sometimes incur high expenses, considerable pain, and inconvenience and end up in a worse condition than before their operation.

What we have seen, then, is a whole series of contingent actions and outcomes. When we sort out all these alternative actions and outcomes, we end up with many possible combinations. How should we make a choice of actions? As in the agenda decision, described in Chapter 5, we should construct a decision tree, inserting our own estimates of costs, values, and probabilities in each specific case. In that way we can decide, on an explicit, logical basis, how much effort to devote to a search for causes.

CLASSES OF CAUSES

We have treated all causes as if they were essentially alike, defining them as factors that affect, influence, alter, or determine some phenomenon. But causal influences are not at all homogeneous. They take many forms.

By sorting out the different kinds of things we may be looking for, we can suggest the occasions when we are likely to find the cause and when it probably will elude us. Also, we can develop sophistication in evaluating the evidence in any particular situation that will help avoid a mistaken interpretation of the facts. The classification of causes set forth in this section is intended to help businesspeople who are beset by puzzling difficulties.

Simultaneous vs. Successive Causes

Causal relationships are best depicted as a "causal net," which illuminates two very important characteristics of causal influences: first, some factors operate simultaneously and in combination with others to determine the behavior of a phenomenon at any given time; and second, each of these influences is, in turn, determined by other influences.

To illustrate this, let us return to the decline in appliance sales in Milwaukee. A senior sales executive in the firm should be able to identify many factors that might "cause" such a sales decline. Each of the items listed in the causal net can be viewed both as a cause of the level of sales and as a consequence of other causes. Sales might be affected by the firm's advertising efforts; these are affected, in turn, by appropriations for advertising, by prevailing charges by advertising media, by talent, and so forth; the advertising appropriation would, in turn, reflect the firm's earnings and presumably would be influenced by the attractiveness of the advertising programs developed by its advertising staff.

What we have illustrated is a chain of events or actions or decisions that are related causally and sequentially — both in timing (certain ones precede and give rise to others) and in direction of influence (usually, each cause influences subsequent events). By contrast, some causes are concurrent. They operate on the same level, simultaneously and collectively, to determine some phenomenon — sales in this case. In combination, they all impinge directly on sales. These are termed "simultaneous causes."

Awareness that causes can operate on different levels can help avert a common error. For example, a research report explaining why the sales by small retailers of appliances have declined in Milwaukee might indicate that (1) fewer calls have been made by the distributor; (2) the retailers show less loyalty to the firm's brand; (3) the salespersons in the stores know less about the brand's product features than was assumed; and (4) the firm's products were given poor position in the stores.

The executive might conclude that he cannot correct the problem because so many causes need correction. Actually, each of these apparent causes may be manifestations of the same underlying cause — neglect of the small retailers by the distributor — and not independent and separate causes of the sales decline. By eliminating one cause, the executive would presumably (in time) eliminate all of them.

Stable/Consistent Causes vs. Unstable/Erratic Causes

Certain influences that determine business phenomena behave in the same way over time, whereas others are inconsistent and erratic. As a general rule, physical forces (chemical, electronic, mechanical, and so on) behave now just as they did in the distant past; they are ordinarily measurable and observable, and we can therefore generally predict their effects.

Erratic influences generally involve social, psychological, political, and human forces. We do not know very much about the effects of such influences since they seem to be unstable over time and to vary substantially in what appear to be similar situations. Whereas we can often quite reliably diagnose difficulties where physical forces are at fault, when nonphysical forces give rise to a difficulty, a causal search is very likely to fail. Unstable influences are just more difficult to understand and predict.

On the whole, physical forces operate within the production sphere, whereas social and psychological forces dominate in marketing and personnel problems. Of course, some production problems result from poor supervision, low labor morale, and the like—which are erratic influences. Correspondingly, some physical forces, such as the operation and location of warehouses, operate in marketing problems.

Initiating vs. Facilitating Factors

The distinction between "initiating" (or "active" or "strategic") factors and "facilitating" (or "enabling" or "contributing") conditions often is crucial to someone trying to get at the root of a problem. We saw an illustration of this difference when we tried to explain why Mr. Jones, the factory manager, took to drink. The harsh criticism of his supervisor was an active, sudden, and visible (perhaps "audible" is more accurate) cause, whereas the undermining of his self-confidence by his son occurred slowly and fairly continuously and therefore lacks the usual appearance of a cause. However, in the absence of the man's vulnerability, we have assumed, the supervisor's criticism would *not* have resulted in Mr. Jones's taking to drink. Therefore, his son's behavior must be regarded as one of the major influences responsible for his drinking—that is, as a cause of it.

Many facilitating causes are "surrounding conditions," or what might be considered environmental factors. The environment is constantly changing and may, in combination with nonenvironmental changes, produce difficulties that would not have occurred had the environment not changed. Decision makers tend to concentrate their research on active causes while ignoring possible facilitating circumstances. If they do so, they will exonerate some causes incorrectly or correct only part of the difficulty.

Recorded vs. Unrecorded Influences

Causes might also be classified on the basis of whether they leave a clear record. We know what happened to certain things at different times with considerable accuracy; prices paid for raw materials, the absences of employees, outdoor humidity, and the like are common examples of recorded factors. On the other hand, quality of services rendered to customers, sales representatives' attitudes, and the degree and locus of secret price cutting by rivals are not easily known, even for the recent past. When such things are involved, a decision maker usually cannot gather the reliable evidence needed to determine what factors gave rise to the firm's present difficulties.

Of course, most factors lie between the extremes of being wholly recorded and unrecorded. The closer they are to the "unrecorded" end of the spectrum, the more likely the quest is to be unsuccessful and costly.

Factors That Produce Feedback vs. Factors That Do Not

Causes can be classified by the speed and accuracy of feedback that one receives about a malfunction. When certain phenomena go "out of control," one learns about them very quickly and can investigate the situation promptly – when memories are likely to be fresh and circumstances are similar to those prevailing when the trouble started. For example, production failures sometimes show up when the finished item is tested – perhaps within minutes, and almost certainly hours, of the time the error was made. By contrast, a falloff in employee morale often passes unrecognized for many months.

Where quick and clear feedback occurs, the likelihood of finding the source of a difficulty is relatively great. Of course, to gain the benefits of prompt feedback, we must develop a system that collects and interprets information very promptly.

Start-up vs. Ongoing vs. Wear-out Causes

In an important class of business difficulties, it is helpful to divide causes into three types:

1. Those associated with the initiation of a process or activity, the start-up of a piece of equipment, or the launching of a venture.
2. Those that occur after the initiation period, after all the "bugs" have been eliminated.
3. Those associated with the process of wearing out.

Although this classification of causes is typically applied to machinery failures, it also clearly applies to organizational problems and those of interpersonal relationships.

This set of distinctions helps considerably in diagnosis. Particular kinds of disorders are associated with the start-up period in the life of a process; similarly, if a piece of equipment has reached the stage where parts begin to wear out, the person trying to find the cause of the difficulty usually knows where to look and what to look for. Also, what remedies one would make depends on whether the item that is ailing is just starting its usable life or nearing its end.

HOW TO SEARCH OUT "THE CAUSE" OF A BUSINESS DIFFICULTY

A decision maker seeking the cause of a difficulty usually will find five types of data helpful:

1. Clues that are to be found by a detailed description of the difficulty itself. These usually include the timing, magnitude, and nature of the difficulty. To interpret a clue, one must understand the phenomenon well enough to know what factors potentially could explain the observed difficulty.
2. Recent changes that might account for the difficulty, especially changes that took place contemporaneously with the onset of the difficulty.
3. Models designed to explain the phenomenon. Such a model would help to interpret clues and to isolate those recent changes that might be relevant. It would generate a list of possible suspects, each to be considered separately and in combination with others.
4. Evidence indicating the factors that accounted for similar difficulties in the past.
5. Consequences that usually are associated with the cause, other than the difficulty itself. Almost every "cause" results in several consequences, not only one. Accordingly, if the other expected consequences of a suspected cause were present, that might "confirm" the presence of the cause.

Each of these types of information can help to establish the working cause of a business difficulty. A decision maker need not consider any, let alone all, of these sources; they are not equally valuable in any given situation. However, we should be aware of these different data sources and know how to exploit them.

Clues Found by Describing the Difficulty Itself

In all "whodunits," the sleuth seeks all clues to the crime and usually finds the culprit by drawing the appropriate inferences from the clues. Business sleuths should also try to get possible leads by making a careful analysis of their problems for possible clues.

A careful description of the difficulty besetting the decision maker should include its magnitude, its timing, its form, etc. Beyond this, it should include an indication of related factors that were *not* affected, thus delimiting the difficulty in a way that might suggest its source.*

One could also ask some questions about personnel difficulties in the course of such an analysis. The decision maker should record the implications of each clue listed — that is, he should associate each clue with recent changes and develop hypotheses to account for the clues.

Let us apply this kind of analysis to the Milwaukee sales decline for illustrative purposes. Insofar as we have not been very specific about this hypothetical example, we will make up some facts as we go along.

Our Milwaukee problem (the "crime") clearly consists of disappointing appliance sales. Our task is to describe the firm's sales experience in the hope of learning its cause from its characteristics. We would usually start by pulling apart the firm's sales to see what subgroups it contains. We will assume that the Milwaukee sales of the firm's different appliances (refrigerators, TV sets, stoves) did not fall by equal proportions; specifically, we will assume that sales of major appliances held up better than those of small appliances. Also, sales in outlying districts fell more than those in midtown; sales of small retailers were off more than those of large ones; and stores with good credit records experienced less of a sales decline than those classified as "slow payers."

We can now analyze other dimensions of the sales decline. In particular, when did it occur? By concentrating on the products whose sales declined most, we might uncover a precise time that sales began to fall. In this example, timing would not be revealing if the trouble resulted from the distributor's neglect of small accounts, because it would not be reflected in lower sales for some time.

---

* For a specific form that gives order and system to the arranging of clues to business problems, see Charles Kepner and Benjamin Tregoe, *The Rational Manager*, New York: McGraw-Hill, 1965, p. 75.

One question that often should be asked about business problems is who is "responsible" for the activity that is in trouble. For example, we might find that the sales representatives who served the retail accounts whose sales declined are not the ones who served the accounts that were performing up to and beyond expectations. In that case, the problem would not seem due to the distributor, who was responsible for selling to all accounts, not only to those whose sales declined.

Let us assume the evidence suggests that (1) the sales decline represented a gradual erosion, not a sharp dramatic drop; (2) the decline was not associated with any unusual complaints by customers, servicemen, or sales representatives; and (3) the problem was most acute among small retailers, especially those in outlying districts. We need to find influences—concurrent changes—that could account for those conditions.

A very experienced executive would have met similar situations before and would realize that the conditions described reflect a fairly clear case of distributor neglect. However, it is possible that the executive responsible for this problem does not interpret the configuration of clues as distributor neglect. What other forms of information might be sought in a search for causes?

Recent Changes That Might Account for the Difficulty

Most people attribute their trouble to some new development—something unusual that happened around the same time the difficulty appeared. Business decision makers usually ask their associates whether anything has happened recently that might explain the difficulty. Sometimes they ask specific questions, especially when they have a hunch. A marketing executive who learns that the firm's market share has dropped sharply in a particular maket might ask immediately whether price cutting has appeared in that market of late or whether the distributor has had any particular trouble with his or her sales representatives or usual sources of credit.

Although some changes that might explain a difficulty are recorded in a firm's information system, this is not typically the case. Usually a decision maker must conduct a special search for information. Unfortunately, it is rarely possible to obtain a complete and reliable list of all potentially relevant changes, no matter how hard one tries. So decision makers' efforts will usually be restricted to getting evidence about only those factors that they suspect are the cause of the trouble.

In the Milwaukee example, one might elicit remarks about the distributor's spending lots of time at the racetrack. Beyond such pertinent information, the sales manager would doubtless learn many things that had happened during the period of disappointing sales but had nothing whatsoever to do with the low sales. It is the decision maker's ability to sift the relevant from the chaff that will largely determine the value of such information.

When an extraordinary change closely matches the characteristics of the difficulty, a decision maker may have all the evidence needed to find a working cause. However, the ability to draw such conclusions depends on an understanding of the phenomenon around which the problem revolves; in short, the decision maker would need a valid model and would also have to know how to employ it.

Suspected Causes Deduced from an Explanatory Model

Models provide understanding. Indeed, they often explain how the different aspects of a phenomenon interact. A model for diagnostic purposes indicates the possible suspects —a valuable starting point for all sleuths. Often the number of suspects is extremely large, however, and not all suspects are equally suspect. What makes a suspect particularly suspicious in any specific case?

Some crimes reflect a special style—a general configuration of circumstances; one would therefore match the suspects against the combination of clues to the crime. But what is involved in this matching process?

Things match because we perceive connections between them. They match from a particular standpoint that we, the observers, read into the situation. A diagnostic (causal) model represents a powerful tool for finding causes when it is combined with relevant data pertaining to sudden changes, similar difficulties in the past, or the presence of other consequences of a suspected cause.

Causes of Similar Difficulties in the Past

Difficulties tend to recur with some frequency; the same symptoms usually result from the same causes. Since history does often repeat itself, decision makers are wise to review history when they face a puzzling difficulty. Unfortunately, it is easy to conclude that a present difficulty is the same as one in the past when that is not the case.

Few business executives are historically oriented; their jobs and temperaments mainly force them to face the future. To identify working causes found for similar situations in the past, an executive might use memory, a solicitation of recollections from others, or a written log. Whatever the source, the use of past experience to diagnose present difficulties depends mainly on being able to associate the current disorder with particular past troubles *that really are similar*. Such parallels can be drawn reliably only by identifying the essential characteristics of the present difficulty and seeking out past troubles that contain the same features.

Presence of Other Consequences of a Suspected Cause

Some causes of difficulties cannot be observed directly; this holds especially for problems involving the behavior of individuals. Resentment, pessimism, misunderstanding, or jealousy can be present without being directly observable; such motives and emotional states must be inferred indirectly from behavior. Also, some causes occur and then disappear; one must find their traces long after they have vanished. Here, other consequences of the cause may provide a clue.

Let us be specific. Assume that some "selective" secret price cutting took place in a market for which an executive is responsible. Assume the product is a supply item, like grinding wheels or paint. Typically, the executive would recognize the loss of more customers than usual only a considerable period after the event. Even if price cutting were a likely suspect, how could that suspicion be verified?

First, one might ask customers why they switched to different suppliers. Second, one might try to examine the invoices sent by the suspected price-cutter to the lost customers. The first option is unreliable because some people would conceal the truth—out of loyalty to the price-cutter, because secret price cutting is of dubious legality, or because they might want a price reduction from the executive's own company. The second option would be possible only through a "leak." So, if an executive is to determine whether the loss of business resulted from a competitor's secret price concessions, other means will usually have to be employed.

One thing to do is to ponder the different consequences of secret price cutting—the things that are likely to be associated with it, beyond a loss of some business. One such piece of evidence would be an allegation by other customers that they were offered price cuts. A second clue is complaints by other rivals that they are being hurt by price cutting. Another is a change in behavior of customers who were lost; for example, they might show some evasiveness toward the company's sales representatives. As with the other four types of data, this source of clues is dependent on the models held by the sleuth.

Identification of Causes by Statistical Analysis

In the sleuthing methods we have discussed, the unique facts in each case require close attention if a decision maker is to find the cause. Most executive decisions involve problems of this type. However, some business problems permit or require different techniques. Difficulties that recur with frequency — for example, out-of-stocks, absenteeism, or rate changes — are a common type in most organizations. In such cases, an executive can employ the techniques of the researcher and statistician rather than those of the detective.

Recurrent difficulties ordinarily reflect some defective underlying arrangement or some fallacious concept; that is, they are an enduring situation rather than an unexpected outside development. In such situations, decision makers can analyze many similar difficulties that occurred in order to uncover their source. A highly detailed analysis of each individual situation is usually not necessary. However, a statistical analysis of many cases does require that decision makers or researchers first become thoroughly acquainted with the details of a few individual situations in an effort to identify the many factors at work and the way they interact.

With the information and understanding thus gained, researchers analyze data for a large number of cases in order to test their hypotheses about the causes of malfunction. They seek the "weight" of large numbers of cases to avoid the errors that can result from accident or chance. Although almost anything can happen once, a relationship that holds time and again cannot easily be dismissed.

Of course, even when statistical techniques are employed, causal analysis is fraught with possibilities for error. In fact, a well-recognized category of errors in causal analysis is known as "nonsense correlations." This phrase refers to phenomena that appear — statistically — causally related when in fact no connection exists among them.

A famous example of nonsense correlations is the following. A "scientist" wanted to test the effects of drinking water on behavior. He did not like water, so he decided to test it in combination with other liquids. He tried water with scotch and got drunk. He tried it with bourbon and got drunk. He used rye with the same effect. So he concluded that water had an intoxicating effect.

Researchers become committed to theories, as other people do, and often settle for highly superficial evidence, failing to employ the powerful techniques at their disposal when working with large numbers of cases. Perhaps the most common and serious error is failure to search out relevant intervening associated variables. Consider the following simple example.

The production department of ABC Corporation has regularly experienced poor output on its Saturday and evening shifts. These shifts are run only from time to time when inventories have been depleted by unexpectedly heavy sales. The workers hired to work those shifts are "casual workers" — often elderly men and housewives who desire only part-time work, cannot easily find other employment, or have been laid off from other jobs.

Management is certain that its low output on such shifts results from the use of "low-quality" workers. By accident — that is, without intending to improve output — management changes the supervisor on the Saturday and evening shifts. What follows is a substantial jump in output, making those shifts more productive than the regular ones. Some judicious inquiries reveal that the regular foreman treated the workers as incompetents and unreliable people. The new foreman is fond of the workers, and they are fond of him. The workers show themselves to have skills and inclination to do at least as well as the company's regular employees.

Statistical analysis of large numbers of cases usually makes possible the test of different combinations of circumstances and the grouping of cases that are similar in all significant respects. This is achieved mostly by simple classification and cross-tabulation, but it also requires an ability to understand what nonobvious factors (such as the foreman's attitude in the preceding example) may be operating as intervening variables.

Causal analysis by statistical means is generally possible only for relatively low-level business difficulties. And usually its use is limited to production, inventory, and logistical difficulties. A growing dimension of statistical analysis is the use of controlled experiments to determine causal relationships. The problems of top management, however, mainly require what we have called "sleuthing."

Summary

The quest for causes is a difficult and complicated process, because most business difficulties are caused by a combination of factors. Phenomena are what they are because of their own essential nature and the character of the particular environment in which they occur, as well as because of what we usually think of as "causal factors." Usually, we cannot find *the* cause of our most vexing problems.

However, it is not always necessary to isolate a cause in order to remove the difficulty. A difficulty may correct itself; it may disappear for reasons we never find out; we can offset it rather than correct it; or we can start over and create a new situation. In order to decide whether to make a search for a cause, executives should construct a decision tree, inserting their own estimates of costs, values, and probabilities.

By identifying the *kind* of cause we may be looking for, we can often figure out whether the search will be worthwhile. Causes can be classified in a number of ways: simultaneous vs. successive, stable/consistent vs. unstable/erratic, initiating vs. facilitating, recorded vs. unrecorded, feedback-producing vs. producing no feedback, start-up vs. ongoing vs. wear-out. Some data that can help in the quest for causes are clues found by describing the difficulty in detail or by examining recent changes, models, past experiences, or consequences associated with the cause.

Statistical analysis helps where there are large numbers of cases. But even statistical analysis is not infallible, and most top-management problems require the kind of "sleuthing" we have described in this chapter.

7
IDENTIFYING
POSSIBLE
COURSES
of ACTION

What actions the decision maker will consider taking depends on the perceived nature of the problem and of its cause.* For example, if the cause is new, unfamiliar, and puzzling, the executive is likely to seek help from others in coping with it. If the problem seems likely to grow rapidly, the executive will act with great speed and probably will be willing to invest large sums of money to obtain a remedy.

Important dimensions of causes, then, are familiarity, cost to correct, time required to effect a remedy, and whether it is self-correcting, cumulative, or static. Table 1 presents a classification of causes built around these dimensions and indicates the general relation of remedies to different causes.

In our problem of decreased sales in Milwaukee, we would characterize the cause "found" by the VP as fairly familiar, large, and possibly cumulative. In the problem involving

* Here, as in the preceding chapter, we will focus more on problem decisions than on opportunity decisions.

Table 1.   A classification of causes.

	Familiar		Unfamiliar	
	Large	Small	Large	Small
Cumulative	Needs action immediately		Needs out- side help badly	Needs help
Self- correcting				
Static		Minor problem		

heavy drinking of a factory manager, the cause was not familiar, probably major, and possibly cumulative (but also possibly
self-correcting).

A more common type of difficulty can be illustrated by the
shakedown problems of a new machine. One might find that
a bolt was not firmly tightened — a familiar problem and a
small cause (though perhaps of a big difficulty) that is
unchanging. In such a case, the cause points directly to the
remedy: you tighten the loose bolt and see if the machine performs properly.

Some causes have obvious remedies; others are known to
be irremediable in the present state of knowledge; and most
have several possible remedies, not all of equal or known efficacy. Of course, more uncertainty usually exists about the
efficacy of a remedy than about the authenticity of a cause.
Even when we employ a "proven" remedy for a disorder, we
usually recognize that it might not work in this case because
the cause is unlikely to be exactly like others in which the
remedy is known to be effective. One rarely finds complete
uniformity of circumstances in comparable business prob-

lems. Since every problem is unique, some doubt is warranted about the efficacy of any proposed remedy. Nevertheless, quite a few people refuse to accept the insolubility of certain disorders, as many charlatans and quacks have learned to their great profit.

We can therefore make another classification of cause/remedy situations. At one extreme, the executive may have settled on a remedy clearly dictated by the nature of the cause; at the other extreme, a cause may have been found for which no remedy is known. In between are problems for which many remedies are known, but which provide only uncertain relief. Table 2 sums up these differences.

Table 2. Directness of tie between cause and remedy.

Number of alleged remedies		Direct tie with cause	Unclear tie with cause
None			
One	Probably effective		
	Dubious effectiveness		
Two	Probably effective		
	Dubious effectiveness		
Many	Probably effective		
	Dubious effectiveness		

Thus decision makers can take quite dissimilar positions at the conclusion of a search for causes, and these differences bear very directly on whether and how they should attempt to find remedies. Clearly, the probability of finding an effective remedy will vary widely according to whether one has located the cause, what the nature of the cause is, and whether known remedies are available.

Main Characteristics of Remedies

We have considered the directness of the link between causes and remedies and asked whether the causes found usually dictate the actions that the decision maker should take. Although cause and remedy sometimes are tightly linked, typically the decision maker has many reasonable alternative remedies for the problem. In such cases, the decision maker must select among alternatives or decide to live with the problem because it appears to be less painful than the cure.

The chief characteristics of remedies that determine their attractiveness are (1) their *probability* of some success; (2) the *degree* to which they are likely to eliminate the difficulty; (3) the *time* required to effect a cure; (4) their *cost;* and (5) the *number of applications* of the remedy that are required.

The probability of a remedy's success. Although no remedy is absolutely foolproof, some inspire more confidence than others. Unfortunately, data on which to base a probability estimate are largely lacking in business situations; the closest thing to such data usually resides in the experience and memory of specialists and consultants, but even they can produce little systematic evidence that establishes the superiority of one remedy over others. Decision makers would often be wise to keep a log in which they record their problems, their diagnoses, remedies attempted, and results of each remedy, with a discussion of their unintended effects. Such logs, shared with colleagues, could represent a valuable resource for a company.

The degree to which the remedy will eliminate the difficulty. Some remedies only partially cure a difficulty; others make the situation even better than it was before the problem arose. For example, to return the purchase price to dissatisfied customers may remove part of the resentment they may feel toward the firm, but it is not likely to make them more favorably disposed toward the firm than they were at the time of purchase. On the other hand, poor employee attendance and turnover record in a department may be attacked by measures that make that department better in those respects than ever before. What usually happens, though, is that remedies simply restore the original situation.

The time required to effect a cure. Speed is a valuable characteristic of a remedy. Ordinarily, difficulties impose costs or pain, or both, and should be eliminated as promptly as possible. But not infrequently, a speedy cure is especially costly and may involve greater risk of failure. For example, summarily firing an employee who has a drinking problem may speedily remove the disorder (the supervisor's malaise) but may cause disruption in the department and incur sizable replacement costs as well.

The cost of the remedy. Naturally, no businessperson can afford to ignore cost and say, "I must have the best remedy possible; money is no object." The cost of a remedy must be balanced against what it is expected to deliver. Unfortunately, some people beset by a problem react emotionally to it and fail to seek this balance. Such people should be careful to consider whether the remedy will seem sensible after the excitement and immediate pain of the problem have come to pass.

The number of applications required. Some remedies cure the difficulty once and for all; others require continuous actions to overcome the difficulty, and when those actions cease, the difficulty recurs. Between these extremes, we find some remedies that require a few or periodic applications. Of course, one would ordinarily prefer the once-only remedy, but that might involve a far higher cost than the "grease it, tighten the connections, and sharpen the edges every two weeks" kind of remedy.

Table 3 presents a matrix that distinguishes remedies by

all of the characteristics discussed above, except for probability of their success. This matrix is so constructed that those remedies that come closest to the upper left-hand corner are most valuable and those in the lower right-hand corner have lowest value.

Table 3.   The value of different types of remedies.

	Degree and speed of improvement attainable							
	Better than before		Full restoration		Improved but not restored		Temporary improvement	
	Fast	Slow	Fast	Slow	Fast	Slow	Fast	Slow
Single action								
Inexpensive	(most val.)							
Costly								
Multiple action								
Inexpensive								
Costly								
Continuous application								
Inexpensive								
Costly								(least val.)

This matrix could be helpful in forecasting the value of remedies the decision maker is likely to find after a search. Experienced decision makers can usually infer from the nature of the difficulty the class of remedy on which they will have to rely.

WHERE TO TURN FOR REMEDIES FOR
BUSINESS DIFFICULTIES

After we have isolated the cause of a problem, we usually have a general idea of the *type* of remedy we will need, yet we are often stuck right at that point. Where, specifically, are we to look for the proper solution? Which sources of remedies are usually most fruitful and reliable? Which are most likely to produce imaginative approaches to difficulties that cannot be overcome by routine methods?

The most common remedy sources are the decision makers themselves, outside people, and "the literature." Among the many factors that determine which source we will turn to are the following: potential damage that might result from the difficulty; the amount of our previous experience with similar difficulties; the availability of an associate who has specialized knowledge of that problem; the danger that the difficulty will speedily grow worse if not remedied promptly; the presence of an outside specialist who is familiar with the background and is available at reasonable cost; and the confidentiality of the problem.

Since this book is devoted mainly to decision makers themselves as a source of remedies, let us merely note here that their best resource is their own memory and then go on to examine the other two options in more detail. First, how can the business decision maker make the best use of specialists, consultants, and other outsiders?

Here are a few suggestions.

1. Senior executives should develop a "stable" of outsiders and gather information about their competence, experience, integrity, availability, and willingness to exert themselves in an emergency. (Sometimes you need such people at the last minute.) They can sometimes be found inside the organization, although they may be outside the particular department affected by the problem.

2. Members of this stable should be given special assignments from time to time to provide them with the background needed to deal competently with problem situations.

3. Arrangements should be made with these outsiders, especially those who charge high fees, which permit casual telephone contacts at modest cost.

4. Funds devoted to outside specialists should be consciously balanced against the sums paid in salary to full-time executives. Access to an effective stable of specialists reduces the need for highly competent and specialized full-time executives who can deal with exceptional and perplexing circumstances and permits emphasis on more commonly available and inexpensive managerial attributes.

One should keep in mind, however, that it is often difficult to find very good consultants. Furthermore, the problem of evaluating consultants' work once you have tried them should not be underestimated (knifing of a consultant by your colleagues is a danger that is not often discussed).

When should an executive seek outside help from published writings rather than from an individual?

Naturally, it is usually far cheaper to get knowledge from an article than from a consultant — if you know such an article exists and can find it. The probability of obtaining concrete assistance with business difficulties from the literature varies enormously with the nature of the problem and the familiarity of the decision maker with the literature. It is all too likely that we will make or authorize an intensive search of the literature and (1) find nothing useful after a very long search, or (2) find something that is invalid or misleading.

Just as some consultants exaggerate their competence, authors sometimes make unfounded statements, invent facts, and reach illogical conclusions; the caliber of business articles and books varies enormously. And, apart from competence, there is a wide range of differences in the relevance of written materials to practical problems. The case histories that are found in books and articles are often less helpful than interesting; they tend to be idiosyncratic and not rich enough in detail to indicate whether all of the relevant variables were considered. Also, there is a widespread tendency for executives who write about their past problems to make them appear more troublesome than was the case and to depict their solutions as more ingenious and effective than the facts would warrant.

Business does not possess a literature like that found in the field of medicine. Medical articles routinely describe disorders, their symptoms, and suggested treatments and contain a review of the effects of different types of treatment and references to experimental evidence. In part, the deficiency of the business literature results from the proprietary interest business executives feel in any remedies they have uncovered at substantial cost to themselves; in greater measure, it results from the lack of a tradition among business managers to consult the literature for help.

All things considered, an executive facing a puzzling difficulty will not often find a solution from a search of the literature. Business literature is helpful mainly in indicating useful general approaches, providing models that can be adopted, and suggesting the names of people to consult in an emergency. In the case of both books and articles, the help that business literature provides is mainly in the form of general understanding rather than specific advice.

Attacking Specific Problems

The area of business decisions is fraught with uncertainty. In one typical kind of situation, we doubt that we have truly found the cause of our difficulty; we are not certain that the cause has not already been corrected by someone else, or has corrected itself; we aren't sure that we could find a good remedy, even if one exists, that would improve the situation;

we don't know whether the remedy we might find would fully restore the situation preceding the onset of the difficulty; and we don't know whether the remedy would require a single action or many. This is, in fact, a fairly accurate description of the Milwaukee problem.

What does a decision maker do in a case like this? Among the alternatives — some of which were discussed in the previous chapter — are the following:

1. Do nothing — just live with the difficulty. (This course of action is singularly unsuited where the difficulty is major or will grow worse unless corrected.)
2. Apply the best-known remedies to each of the possible causes in some carefully selected sequence. (One might adopt first the remedies that are quickest and cheapest to apply, or one might sequence the remedies according to the frequency with which they corrected similar difficulties in the past.)
3. Apply many remedies at once.
4. Start over — replace the troublesome person or machine — if that can be done.
5. Get rid of part of the troublesome situation.

In a sense, a situation in which so much uncertainty exists is unique; yet here are a few very general suggestions that might help people who face such a situation.

First, array the potential remedies for each of the suspected causes and try to estimate the probabilities of success and the degree of improvement that each will produce (assuming that each suspected cause is a real one). In short, what outcomes should be expected from each potential remedy?

A careful examination of the prospects may indicate that you should just live with the situation and/or try to offset it, wait for it to correct itself, start over, or try the possible remedies until the trouble is eliminated.

Second, evaluate the need for speed. If the value of speed is great, you will generally opt for a program of attacking several causes at once. Technological considerations will often indicate which attempted remedies fit together best. Not infrequently, several remedies can be tried at once at about the same cost as a single remedy; for example, once a machine has been disassembled, several suspect parts can be replaced or lubricated or sharpened at little more cost than that required to replace or lubricate or sharpen only one.

Of course, when you apply many remedies at once, you cannot know which remedy worked, and you may thus lose information that could prove valuable in the future. In terms of costs and benefits, however, future use is usually of low value when speed is an important consideration.

Third, order the remedies in a sequence in which they might best be applied. Put at the top of the list those that would work quickly (if at all), are inexpensive and easy, and have no likely side effects, and save for last those remedies for which the opposite is true.

Let us now apply this kind of reasoning to the sales problem in Milwaukee. Let us assume that at the conclusion of his search for causes, the VP was still puzzled about the source of the sales decline. He believed that the distributor's behavior probably contributed to the trouble, and although he doubted that the distributor was fully to blame for the failure to meet sales goals, he worried lest the distributor's performance deteriorate further and cause more serious difficulties in the Milwaukee market.

Let us further assume that he resolves to do something about improving his distributor situation, whether or not the distributor is responsible for the current sales problem. Also, let's assume he knows that one or more of his competitors have been running strong promotions that he thinks (but does not know for sure) are effective. He also believes that certain rival brands have won increased customer favor in the Milwaukee market and that part of the sales problem resulted from bad luck and accident. In such a situation, how does he proceed?

First, carefully avoiding the error of jumping to conclusions, he prepares a list of the causes that *might be* operating: failings of the distributor, successful promotion by a rival, increased popularity of another brand, and bad luck.

Taking the distributor problem first, he decides that just living with the difficulty would result in a worsening of the situation, so that option is out. He then dredges his memory in an effort to find situations in the past that were more or less parallel. Can he remember previous instances in which a distributor was falling down on the job and in which he applied remedies that worked? Or has he read any articles that addressed themselves to similar situations?

In both these cases, memory seems an inadequate tool. The reasons for weaknesses of distributors vary, and it is unlikely that exactly the same factors that applied in similar situations in the past will apply now. Also, in the past our decision maker could have selected a remedy that did not get at the true cause. For example, he may have observed an improvement in sales that was actually general throughout the market and did not represent superior performance by his distributor, and then attributed the improvement to what was actually a remedy for a mistaken cause. (As we have noted, it is extremely difficult to obtain reliable feedback on remedies applied to business problems, especially if they were tried some time in the past.) Further, in scanning his memory bank for helpful articles, the VP fails to find any models that fit this situation.

He could, he reasons, get rid of all or part of the problem by replacing the distributor, but as the market research director pointed out, that would cost $40,000. Determining whether this would be a good investment or a waste would require an analysis of the cause of the cause — the *reason* the distributor might be failing and the possible effects of such approaches as direct confrontation or paying for psychological help.

The VP then turns to the other potential causes and their related possible remedies. How about countering the strong promotion by a rival distributor? There seem to be possibilities here. Like most marketing executives, the VP has a kit of pet strategies that he has found to be effective for stimulating sales. He could try to persuade the distributor to run a major promotion around a favorite theme of his — cooperative advertising allowances for retailers, point-of-sale materials that would be provided free to the retailers, give-away merchandise for customers, or price reductions on particular models in the line.

However, he does believe that the distributor's behavior contributed to the trouble in Milwaukee, and he doubts that this particular distributor could be expected to execute an imaginative sales promotion. Would not the time and money that his company would be forced to invest in such a promotion produce a bigger increase in sales if devoted to other markets where the distributors are skilled in promotion and eager to apply their skill? That is, shouldn't the company bet on winners rather than try to bail out losers? Reasoning in this manner, the VP decides that running a promotion simply to counteract his rival's efforts might not be a suitable remedy.

He goes on to consider how he might cope with a shift in customer preference believed to result from superior product features of competitive brands. Presumably, the most direct remedy would be to have his company imitate the features, or add other attractive product features, in the coming year's models. But that solution would be slow, and it would also be more appropriate for a general loss of business to this rival throughout the country than for the Milwaukee sales difficulty.

Bad luck is the next cause for which the VP tries to list a remedy. Unfortunately, he knows no remedies for bad luck. Unlike the other causes, this one (if it in fact exists) would just have to be lived with.

The best possibilities for corrective action, then, appear to lie in the areas of the distributor's behavior and the promotion of sales. Both types of measure together might help correct the difficulty or at least slow the decline in sales.

Initiating a new promotion plan might be useful in itself — that is, boost sales — even if the rival's promotion was not the true or most important cause. The main problem facing the VP would be his opportunity costs — the things for which he might use his resources instead of applying them to Milwaukee. Possibly, by taking action in other markets he would obtain a far better overall increase in sales and profits. He would want to balance that possibility against the risk that if he allowed the downturn in Milwaukee to continue for long, his brand would deteriorate in value and many important retailers would become disenchanted with it. To evaluate possible courses of action, he might use a decision tree, as we have indicated in other chapters.

All the remedies the VP has considered are, to an experienced marketing executive, more or less routine; that is, they have been tried by marketing executives before. Usually, tried-and-true solutions are sufficient for business difficulties of this sort. But it is possible that our decision maker will decide to seek a novel, untested solution. This will require a certain amount of creativity, which will be the subject of a later chapter.

SUMMARY

The quest for causes does not always point to any particular solution. Often we will find ourselves still enmeshed in uncertainty, not knowing for sure whether we have found the cause(s) or whether it is possible to improve the situation. Still, the action we take will depend on how we perceive the causal situation, and the effectiveness of the solution will usually depend on its relationship to the cause.

In selecting a remedy, the chief characteristics we will (or should) consider are the probability of some success, the degree to which the proposed remedy is likely to eliminate the difficulty, the time it will require, the cost, and the number of applications that are going to be necessary. Our choice of a remedy will also be influenced by a number of other factors, including the potential damage that might result if the difficulty is not corrected, the amount of our experience with similar difficulties, our knowledge of the background of this particular situation, and the availability of appropriate outside resources.

Our own memory and experience are the most common sources of remedy ideas, since most problems are of the sort that have been corrected by us or by others in the past. Other sources are associates or outside specialists and business literature. Executives would be wise to keep a "stable" of experts who can be called on in an emergency and who can give temporary help at low cost. Business literature is generally of little help in an emergency situation; its value lies more in indicating general approaches and names of people to consult than in providing specific advice.

To select one or several remedies from a collection of possibilities, we might first list the remedies for each of the suspected causes and estimate the outcomes of each. We will then want to evaluate the need for speed, consider which possible remedies fit best together, and order the remedies in a sequence in which they might best be applied — with the easy and inexpensive ones at the top of the list. A decision tree can be helpful in evaluating possible outcomes.

8

FORECASTING: SYSTEMATIC SUBJECTIVISM

Once you have received a signal that a decision should be made, added the item to your agenda, found a working cause, and identified some possible courses of action, the next step is to select the best course of action. In order to do this, you need some idea of the results of the various possible actions. To achieve this, you need to forecast. When you manipulate a model in order to look at certain possible outcomes of a decision, you're using a form of forecasting.

Executive decision makers cannot possibly have all the information that would be ideal in order to forecast an outcome. In fact, the information they would like to help them make choices is often difficult and costly to obtain, if not entirely nonexistent. And no matter how long they wait and how much they spend to obtain additional data, an information gap is inevitable. That does not mean, of course, that they can or should refrain from making decisions because of lack of information. At some point, they must go ahead and make the decisions based on more or less insufficient hard data.

The higher up the managerial ladder the executive is, the wider the information gap is likely to be. At lower levels, decisions tend to be more of the "programmed" type: delineated, limited, and repetitive. At higher levels, decisions are broader and have more to do with future events. Rather than following precedent, these higher-level decisions tend to *set* precedent, and thus there is no existing model that fits precisely.

Guesswork

Faced with the necessity of making choices with less knowledge of the consequences of each alternative than we would like to have, what are we to do?

One thing almost all decision makers do at one time or another is to simply make guesses. They rely on "hunches" or "intuition" to substitute for the information required. Sometimes this procedure works surprisingly well. Researchers at the New Jersey Institute of Technology* studied groups of top executives to determine their amount of precognitive ability — a form of extrasensory perception. It was found that some executives had more precognitive ability than others; that is, they were better able to anticipate the future intuitively. The researchers also discovered that those top managers with the highest precognitive ability had the strongest positive effect on their companies' profit picture.

Other experiments have demonstrated that human subjects do well at estimating certain kinds of probabilities and not so well at estimating others.† The kinds of events they do

---

* See John Mihalasky, "ESP in Decision Making," *Management Review*, April 1975, pp. 32–37.

† For a discussion of some of these experiments see Ward Edwards, Lawrence D. Phillips, William L. Hays, and Barbara C. Goodman, "Probabilistic Information Processing Systems: Design and Evaluation," *IEEE Transactions on Systems, Science and Cybernetics*, September 1968, pp. 248–255.

best with are those that can be estimated on the basis of logic or extensive personal experience. That certainly seems reasonable enough. What is more useful for decision makers to know is the areas in which their estimates are likely to be off. Subjective estimates have been found to be characterized by systematic errors. For example, people systematically overestimate the likelihood of events that have a small probability (with an actual value of about one chance in seven or less) and systematically underestimate large probabilities (with a true value of about seven in eight). This tendency is called the "over-under effect."

These experiments also demonstrate the relative inability of the executive to manipulate inputs of new information. When it comes to revising probabilities on the basis of new information, human subjects are consistently and systematically conservative.

These conclusions are based on a whole series of experiments, ranging from very simple to very complex. A simple example might involve showing the subject two urns, which he is told contain red and white balls. One urn has 75 percent red balls and 25 percent white; the other has 75 percent white balls and 25 percent red. The subject is told this but he does not know which urn is which. One of the urns is selected by the toss of a coin.

At this point, the probability is .5 that the selected urn has 75 percent red balls, and this the subject readily comprehends. Then new information is added: a random sample of five balls is drawn from the selected urn. The sample contains four red balls and one white ball. The subject is now asked to estimate the probability that the selected urn has 75 percent red balls.

Here, the subject has been given a straightforward kind of sampling information that clearly enhances the likelihood that the selected urn has 75 percent red balls. By how much?

Most subjects estimate the probability as about .75 or .8. In fact, it is more than .96. This kind of underestimation of the effect of new information in changing the probabilities of hypotheses is pervasive.

The results of such experiments are particularly germane to business decision problems because many business decisions take precisely this form: one starts with estimates of the probabilities of two or more conditions, and these estimates are to be revised as additional information is received.

For example, in a decision to market or not to market a new product, the condition of concern might be somewhat crudely lumped into two possibilities — high demand and low demand — with initial estimated probabilities. The use of test markets would provide information that could be used to form revised estimates of these probabilities. Since this is exactly the kind of situation described in the various experiments, the cited results strongly suggest that when such revisions are made after the test marketing, the estimates are likely to be quite far off the mark, erring on the side of conservatism.

However, in addition to the phenomenon known as the "conservatism of probabilistic information processing," there is another strange prevalent error. This error results from a confounding of probabilities and values: large numbers of people seem to simultaneously assume that a very unpleasant event that has a small probability will not occur, but that a pleasant event with the same probability very well may. This asymmetrical bias tends to result in overoptimistic views of hazardous projects.

Both these biases should be taken into consideration when a decision such as whether to market or not needs to be made. But *how* does one take such factors into consideration? This is a very subjective process. Is there any way to make subjectivism systematic?

The best way to do this is to make the subjective estimates as explicit as possible. In this way it is easier to utilize the judgments of people with diverse viewpoints.

In the case we have just mentioned, the decision maker may conclude, on the basis of revised estimates, that the product should be marketed. Suppose the decision maker would like the opinions of other competent executives. If one of them disagrees and thinks the product should not be marketed, it is not very helpful for that person to say, "Well, I guess I just don't agree with you—it doesn't feel right to me." If each person makes subjective estimates of the various quantities needed and communicates these estimates and their rationale to the other, it is a lot easier to determine who is correct. The two executives may differ in their selection of a final course of action because, say, one of them gives a higher probability to a high level of demand for the new product. In discussing the reasons for the disagreement, they may discover that one of them has information that the other lacked.

Also, since human beings apparently do well at estimating the probabilities of various bits of information but do poorly at revising the probabilities of the hypotheses on the basis of added information, the experimenters suggest that the people who assess the basic probabilities should not be involved with the revisions of the probabilities. In this way the executives whose opinions are sought will not have the original bias of the decision maker. The decision problem will have been broken down into two more easily manageable parts.

PREDICTING OUTCOMES

For executives who are making decisions on their own, there are some valuable tools that aid in making subjectivism more systematic. One of these is the decision tree, which, as we have seen, is useful in making agenda decisions as well as decisions further down the line. When decision trees are used, the forecasting process consists of (1) predicting possible outcomes, (2) assigning values to these possible outcomes, and (3) estimating the probabilities of these outcomes.

Let us look first at the question of listing possible outcomes. In many decision problems, particularly those with a small number of possible courses of action, it appears quite simple to list all the outcomes that might result. For example, the problem of whether or not to market a new product may be adequately summarized if the various possible levels of sales are taken as the outcomes. However, even in these seemingly easy cases the simplicity may be more of an illusion than a reality. Thus, in our example, the relevant states of the world might be the possible demand levels for the new product, and the outcome might be the sales that would be obtained from a given demand level as determined by the size of the plant that would be constructed to produce the new product.

It usually requires considerable knowledge and insight to envisage all the possible important effects or outcomes of any action. Almost any action has many effects, and these effects often have various effects of their own. It is often these effects of effects that are overlooked in listing outcomes. Is there anything that can be done to help avoid overlooking relevant outcomes?

The executive will probably only be successful in identifying all possibilities when one or both of two conditions are fulfilled: first, there must be a stable environment for the decision problem; second, the forces that are operating must be thoroughly understood. These are clearly interrelated, because when the forces that act are stable, one accumulates experience with them that often permits thorough understanding. Also, one cannot easily disentangle the effects of factors that operate in a highly dynamic environment. This granted, it is still worth discussing these two requirements separately.

An environment is considered stable if it has behaved consistently and with discernible pattern in the past and if there is good reason to expect the past patterns to persist into the future. It does not require knowledge of the forces that determine the behavior of the environment to conclude that the environment is stable — although such knowledge would help. For example, the factors that cause radioactivity are not known, but there is every reason to believe that atomic disintegrations will continue to occur in a stable way. However, when the forces are not known it is easy to conclude incorrectly that stability will continue. Thus, for decades telephone usage and the demand for new telephones were cited as clear examples of stable phenomena. Yet some important changes took place in the late 1960s that caused the whole pattern to change, and forecasts of demand levels turned out to be quite wrong.

A valid model certainly helps explain what happens, and it should aid in predicting outcomes. But here again there are qualifications. First, the determinants of a phenomenon that one wishes to forecast may be as difficult to forecast as the phenomenon itself. For example, if the chief determinant of the number of new telephone installations is the number of marriages and the number of housing starts, then one might find these determinants as difficult to forecast as the number of new telephone installations. If a model is to assist in forecasting, it must build upon factors that are more stable and predictable than the phenomenon to be forecast.

The second qualification is that unless the forces interact in a simple way, the executive is unlikely to be able to predict outcomes without explicit assistance from technical experts. The two major elements that produce complexity are (1) a great number of factors and (2) probabilistic interactions.

Many of the methods of management science and operations research were developed precisely to determine the outcomes in complex cases where the operating forces are known. Sometimes mathematical analysis can be used to deduce the probability distribution of outcomes. Often both steps of the forecast — list of outcomes and probability — are done simultaneously. Even a seemingly simple decision problem such as determining the number of toll booths that should be open at a tunnel is really difficult to resolve without mathematical analysis, because waiting time depends on the amount of incoming traffic, which is itself not a simple factor.

Sometimes a model is so complex that simple mathematical analysis is not sufficient. Suppose, for example, that you are trying to design a model of the alternative futures of a town — one that will take into account the economic, governmental, environmental, and social factors. Only a computer can help you here.

A complicated model that closely approximates a dynamic real-world situation is called a *simulation*. Business games played with the help of a computer are simulations, and so are the models that Jay Forrester designed to forecast possible outcomes of high-level policies on dynamic industrial and urban situations.*

Simulation is particularly useful when the interacting forces can be expressed in a set of mathematical equations. When this is the case, it is possible to use the mathematical equations and a computer to generate the outcomes that would result if the actual system operated over a very long

* *Industrial Dynamics,* Cambridge, Mass.: The M.I.T. Press, 1961.

period of time. The computer can simulate months of operation of the real system in seconds or minutes of computer time. Often the results obtained through simulation show that the effects of certain actions, over a long period of time, will be considerably different from what would have been predicted by traditional means.

Computer simulations have been extremely helpful in predicting outcomes in cases ranging from production scheduling in multiproduct plants to interaction of governmental and social policies. However, simulations can be used only when one assumes a certain stability in the environment and when the interacting forces are known. (*Some* instability can be allowed for by building possible changes into the simulation model.) But the effects of many decisions — particularly high-level ones — take place far in the future, and as the time span increases, it becomes more and more likely that the environment will *not* remain stable and that new forces will be operative. What can be done to forecast outcomes for decision problems such as these?

One promising approach is the construction of scenarios. A scenario is a statement written by an expert or experts which attempts to describe a complex problematic situation and indicate the most plausible outcomes that may result. It is a kind of word picture of some future time, or a play in which a future situation is acted out.

In a scenario only a small proportion of the total possible outcomes is described. But if the author of the scenario is an expert in the necessary disciplines, is thoroughly immersed in the underlying process, and has enough imagination, there is good reason to believe that the scenario will include the most important outcomes.

Scenarios were first developed as a technique for forecasting outcomes of top-level, long-range governmental and military decisions. However, their potential importance in business decision problems is being increasingly recognized, and some large companies are already using them as a standard method for the analysis of their long-range policy decisions. Scenarios are a major technique of the new field called "futurism," which already has journals and dozens of books devoted to it.

VALUES AND INCREMENTALISM*

One of the trickiest parts of forecasting is determining the values of the different possibilities. Business decision makers, as we saw in the chapter on the agenda decision, have to take into account opportunity costs, direct costs, and other costs; also, many "values" — such as an executive's peace of mind — are hard to quantify.

In evaluating the consequences of decisions, there is an important concept that many decision makers overlook. That concept is incrementalism, or incremental analysis, and it serves as an antidote for the almost natural tendency to think in terms of averages. Decision makers who use incrementalism realize that each decision represents an increment — a change from the current situation. The decision maker thinks in terms of added costs and added benefits rather than average costs and average benefits. Added costs and benefits are usually quite different from the average. Let us see why that is true.

The production cost of most products involves a host of individual costs; some are virtually unaffected by changes in the output of the item while many vary in rough proportion to output. Since the unvarying costs ("fixed costs") can be spread over a larger number of units as output expands, the

* See also Appendix B.

average cost of an item will tend to decline with increases in output.

For example, the average production cost of an item at some level of output might be $8.00. The added cost to produce an extra unit when that level of output has been attained might be far less than that—say, $6.00—since it would not require additional payment for many services included in fixed costs. It is this additional cost that the decision maker should take as the relevant figure in all decisions about that last unit. Since incremental costs can differ substantially from the average, decision makers must be suspicious of all averages, particularly those they receive as cost estimates made by the accounting department, which computes many costs for purposes other than decision making.

As another example of incrementalism, let us assume that Dr. Jones contributed $3,000,000 to her prep school to purchase land and build 30 tennis courts. The costs of maintaining the courts for the year are estimated to be $5,000 a month, all year long. However, the girls are in the school for just nine months. A tennis pro from a neighboring city offers to assume 75 percent of the maintenance of the courts for the other three months as his rental payment. The headmaster is sure that there will be no other offers, and there is no other use for the courts. Since the court maintenance is reduced for the school and (in this case) there are no other costs, such as legal fees, to be considered, the school is better off accepting the offer, even though the rental payment does not even cover complete maintenance.

Incremental analysis also helps take into account an extremely important decision variable: time. For many kinds of decisions, the outcomes will have effects over a period of years. The question is how the values over the different years for any one outcome should be consolidated into one value for the outcome. Every executive knows that the procedure to be followed is to discount the yearly values for any one out-come back to the present value. This approach is usually a good one. However, there are two points that should be considered.

First, the discount factor itself should depend partly on the various opportunities available to the decision maker. If the question is how to invest money, the decision will depend on the use that would be made of the dollars. Will a particular investment earn interest? Will it retire long-term debt? Will it reduce short-term debt? Each of these might imply a different discount factor.

Perhaps the most commonly accepted basis for determining the discount factor argues that the dollars could be used in general company activities and ought to earn the same amount as the company generally earns on its capital. This, then, provides a basis for determining the discount factor. Unfortunately, this is a dubious argument. Suppose a company has made a long series of capital investments and that the company always aimed for a return of 20 percent on these investments. Suppose further that some of the decisions turned out to be bad ones and that, as a result, the company is actually earning 16 percent. Should 16 percent be used as the basis for determining the discount factor ($1/1.16 = .8621$), or should the discount factor be based on the goal of 20 percent ($1/1.2 = .8333$)?

The conclusion is that there is no single discount factor that can be unambiguously calculated from company data. The discount factor should depend on the specific alternatives that are available to the company *at the time of the decision* and *throughout the time span of the effects* of the outcomes.

Second, however compelling the logic of discounting values over time, there are cases where this is *not* the most viable approach. For example, suppose two outcomes have dollar values over a five-year time span as follows:

Outcome I: 1, 2, 3, 4, 5
Outcome II: 3, 3, 1, 2, 6

Here Outcome II is preferred to Outcome I for any reasonable discount factor. But let's suppose that the amounts are in millions of dollars and that one of these two outcomes will represent the major part of company earnings over the next five years. Management (and stockholders) might very much prefer Outcome I with its steady growth of returns and the implication of good, careful management.

Although incremental analysis is clearly an insightful way of looking at the consequences of decisions, most business firms still do not compute incremental costs routinely. Consequently, an executive requesting a figure on costs from the appropriate source in the firm will usually not receive a measure of incremental costs. (This difficulty can often be overcome by specifically requesting a computation of "direct" costs.)

A more serious problem arises from the difficulties of measuring incremental costs and revenues when they are intangible. Although no foolproof rules can be established for the valuation of intangible benefits and sacrifices, three lines of approach can help one arrive at satisfactory estimates (systematic subjectivism).

For example, assume that some action under consideration would worsen employee morale for some time. How might this effect be assigned a numerical cost?

One approach would be to estimate the subsequent tangible effects of worsened employee morale in the form of increased labor turnover, higher absenteeism, possible increased militancy of labor, greater risk of strikes, and higher production and administrative costs due to a decline in effort expended by employees. (We recognize that morale is not always related to these effects in the same way; contented workers sometimes are unproductive workers.) In this case, the value assigned to the intangible effect would represent the sum total of the expected tangible adverse effects of the intangible result of the decision.

The second approach to the valuation of intangibles would be to estimate the cost that the firm would be forced to incur to restore employee morale to the level from which it has fallen. Often, a firm might adopt measures that would just offset the adverse results of a decision it has made. A third approach is to have management estimate what it would be willing to spend to avoid the injury to employee morale.

In assigning a numerical value to intangibles, a decision maker would be wise to explore all of these approaches. The value used would normally be the lowest one since management would ordinarily do what was least costly.

Another way to evaluate intangibles is simply to assign values on a scale of ten. Managers using performance appraisal forms do this all the time; although it may seem at first glance that an element such as "willingness to work hard" would be difficult to quantify, it is actually easy to rate someone a "5" or a "7" in this quality. Subjectivism does not have to be capricious.

Estimating Probabilities

In certain types of decisions, such as the agenda decision discussed in Chapter 5, probabilities of various outcomes must be estimated. Again, this is a subjective process but one that lends itself to a systematic approach. For example, the states of the world for a decision to market or not to market a new product might be represented as five different possible demand levels: 1, 3, 5, 7, and 9 millions of dollars per year. The decision maker might make subjective estimates of the probabilities such as:

Sales (millions)	Probability
$1	.2
3	.4
5	.2
7	.1
9	.1

Of course, these are actually guesses. Such guesses are based on the decision maker's past experience plus his or her knowledge of current trends and other environmental influences. Another kind of forecast for the same situation might be $4 million sales with a 50 percent chance that the actual sales will be between $2,250,000 and $5,500,000. This calculation can be made with standard deviation tables.

A probability distribution curve is useful in estimating probabilities when—as in the case of demand levels—there is a large number of possible outcomes. If the possibilities include any demand from 0 to $5 million per year, obviously we do not want to include each of these possible levels on the decision tree. However, we would like to know the probability distribution over all the possible demand levels from 0 to $5 million, because from that distribution we can deduce the probabilities of the demand levels we actually do use on the tree.

Our probability distribution curve might look like Figure 8. For this example the probability of a demand of $3.5 million is about twice as large as the probability of a demand of either $1.5 million or $4.8 million. When such a sketch has been made, all the probabilities—each estimated subjectively—can be determined directly from the graph. This procedure is quite easy to follow if the executive is familiar with the elements of probability theory. Financial analysts usually find it easy to use this approach to obtain their subjec-

Figure 8. Probability distribution curve for a sales problem.

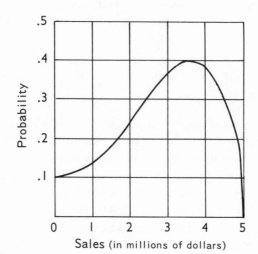

tive probability distributions of earnings per share for the companies they are analyzing.

Although the executive need estimate only a few points on the curve, the more points are determined, the better the approximation to the actual subjective probability distribution will be. However, there are limits to the number of discriminations a person can be reasonably asked to make. Three points are not enough, and more than ten verges on being unreasonable. Five to seven points ought to be adequate in most cases. Note that this has nothing at all to do with the number of outcomes included on the decision tree. We want to determine the probability distribution first and, from it, deduce the probabilities needed on the tree.

There are two basic kinds of approaches that we as decision makers can use. One is to state the question in terms of probabilities and the answer in terms of demand levels. The other is to state the question in terms of demand levels and the answer in terms of probabilities.

An example of the first kind would be: "What is the lowest realistic demand level that I expect? That is, I think there is one chance in twenty that actual demand will be less than *what* level?" An example of the second kind would be: "What do I think the probability is that actual demand will be less than $1 million?"

The first kind of question is the more convenient for deducing the subjective probability distribution. If we want five points, we can use these questions:

1. What is the lowest demand level for which I think there is one chance in twenty that the actual demand will be less than the stated level?
2. What is the demand level for which I think there is one chance in four that the actual demand will be less than the stated level?
3. What is the demand level for which I think there is one chance in two that the actual demand will be less?
4. What is the demand level for which I think there is one chance in four that the actual demand will be greater than the stated level?
5. What is the demand level for which I think there is one chance in twenty that the actual demand will be greater?

Questions of the second kind can then be used as checks on the adequacy of the constructed subjective probability distribution.

We should be careful to guard against the two biases mentioned earlier—the tendency to overestimate small probabilities and the confounding of probabilities and values (assuming that an unpleasant event with a small probability will not happen and a pleasant event with a small probability will).

Once forecasting has been applied to the decision situation, we generally will have a clear choice of actions. Still, it must be remembered that forecasting is far more of an art than a science and most business forecasts are error-prone. Although the names of some of the newer forecasting techniques — periodogram analysis, correlograms, autocorrelation, spectral analysis, exponential smoothing, and so forth — *sound* impressive and scientific, it is a useful antidote to recall that Charles Roos, who devoted most of his life to forecasting problems, once summarized all of these methods under the category of "naive methods." His justification for so doing was that all of them rest on the "naive" assumption that what has been occurring in the past will continue to occur in the future. Therefore, future-oriented forecasting tools such as scenarios and simulations may often be just as useful as precise straight-line mathematical tools. The decision maker must pick the technique or combination of techniques that are best suited to the individual decision problem — and even then he must be aware of the limitations of these tools.

SUMMARY

Forecasting the consequences of a decision is a necessary prerequisite to selecting the best course of action. Yet, since decisions involve the future, executives can never have all the information that would be ideal. Despite the information gap, they must go ahead and make the decisions anyway. It is not necessarily a bad thing to rely partly on hunches or "guess-work," as long as the decision maker is aware of the biases that tend to occur, such as the "over-under effect." The important thing is to make explicit the reasons for the decision, especially if other people are involved in it.

One useful tool for organizing this phase of the decision process into a step-by-step system is the decision tree. In order to build a decision tree, it is necessary to list all possible

outcomes, assign values to each possibility, and (usually) estimate the probability of each outcome.

Identifying all the possibilities (including effects of effects)
can only be done if we have a valid model of the situation and
if the decision environment is stable. Even here, there are difficulties: the variables that determine a phenomenon may be
as difficult to forecast as the phenomenon itself, and the
forces may interact in a very complex way. In the latter case,
operations research and computers may help; computers can
simulate very complex situations. For events that will take
place far in the future — in which case the environment will
probably not remain stable — scenarios can be a useful forecasting device.

In assigning values to the various possibilities, we must
quantify the elements in some way. We can state the lowest acceptable cost and use that as a basic value, or we can evaluate
alternatives on a scale of, say, one to ten. A concept called
incrementalism, which directs us to think in terms of *added*
costs and *added* benefits, is useful because it is an antidote for
the natural tendency to think in terms of averages.

Estimating probabilities can be done by constructing a
subjective distribution curve based on five to seven probabil-
ties. Such a curve will present us with any number of choices
to use on the decision tree.

9

CREATIVITY in DECISION MAKING

We have carried the decision-making process to a fork in the road: one branch leads to a selection of solutions; the other might be followed if we are dissatisfied with courses of action that have been tried before and seek creative, new solutions. An executive who has uncovered what seems to be the working cause of a problem but does not know how to correct it may conduct a creative effort to develop a new remedy. Likewise, an executive who wants to develop new opportunities may employ creative efforts to find untried approaches.

And just what *is* a creative effort? The vice president of marketing and the regional sales manager in Milwaukee are approaching this question. We will eavesdrop on them as they discuss their sales problem.

VP *I take it, then, that we agree that the sales trouble in Milwaukee probably is due to the distributor. It doesn't matter that we won't agree that it is family difficulties which are causing him to perform poorly. All we have to do is take the necessary action to clear up the trouble.*

SM   Before you talk about remedies, let's recognize that the fact that we agree as to the cause of the problem doesn't make us right. And we have a good deal of evidence that there may be more than one cause operating. In particular, I still think there is some price cutting.

VP   *All right, all right, we've been through all that before. But what do we do about our distributor? I vote for giving him notice immediately that his franchise is being canceled. We should immediately start the ball rolling to find his replacement.*

SM   I'm reluctant to do that yet. Oh, I know it's our policy, but we've been wrong with that policy several times. What other things might we do?

VP   *Come on, now; we've spent too much time on this problem already. Let's do what has to be done and get on with some of our other problems. That distributor has gone downhill for over seven months now. We have learned that you can't reform a bad distributor. And that's why we have the policy.*

SM   True enough. Still, we have an unusual case here, and I'm not persuaded that our general policy is appropriate. Surely we aren't limited to only one course of action by our policy?

VP   *We can't reexamine policy every time we come to apply it, can we?*

SM   I see your point, but I think we should question certain policies all the time because they seem to apply in most but not all cases. This is one of those policies, and frankly, I don't think it applies here at all well. Don't we both regret that we changed our Boston distributor two years ago? We spent about $40,000 to make the change and ended up with a worse distributor.

VP   *But that wasn't the fault of the policy. We simply handled the situation badly. We replaced Jones with someone who turned out to be a complete lemon.*

SM   Yes, but it's more complicated than that, because Jones is now the Westinghouse distributor and he's doing a great job for them.

VP   *All right. I give up. You win. But what are you proposing that we do now? I'm willing to try some alternative to our usual policy if you've got a good one. But, frankly, I haven't heard any good suggestions, and I certainly don't have one myself.*

SM   Well, that's hardly surprising. Neither of us has been trying to find a new way to correct our difficulty; so far we've been concentrating on finding the cause of the problem. I don't have a good alternative either—at the moment. But with a little luck and lots of effort we should be able to generate half a dozen ideas on how to salvage this distributor. And I think it's worth the effort to try.

VP   *I really don't think you can generate new ideas just because you try to. At least I can't.*

SM   I don't think you'll ever come up with new ideas unless you try. To me that means that you try hard and under circumstances where you are likely to be creative. Most of us think we've tried if we've given a problem a few minutes' thought. You may find that you're really an idea man if you operate in an environment that's conducive to creativity and set out consciously to generate new ideas.

VP   *I'd label that a creative suggestion and invite you to find a way to attack this Milwaukee problem creatively. Certainly a lot of money is involved, and it would be worth a small investment to see if we could produce some new answers to the recurrent problem of distributors who have fallen down on the job.*

We never know whether we can generate new ideas until we have tried; no reliable method exists for forecasting when the effort to be creative will be successful. On the other hand, since the rewards of creative solutions are often high, we might come out far ahead even if we have numerous failures for each success.

What Is Creativity?

Most people associate creativity with brilliant insights, dramatic discoveries, and poetic flights of imagination — the fruits of genius. The overwhelming weight of evidence, though, indicates that creativity is actually a fairly common resource that can be harnessed and used by executives in nearly every stage in decision making. It can help in constructing signaling systems, developing agendas, building models, measuring intangibles, devising ways of collecting nonobvious information, diagnosing causes, and so forth.

Methods have been devised to increase the output of useful new ideas by people working individually and in groups. Many firms are using these methods, for bright ideas can often be turned into substantial revenue. In order to maximize the creative output of individuals and organizations, it is helpful to know how creativity works and what its symptoms are.

Creativity has been defined as "applied imagination."* The chief characteristics of a creative solution are *usefulness* and *novelty;* that is, it must be applicable to a real-life problem, and it must not be a direct logical extension of the traditional solutions that it resembles most. Of course, creative acts vary widely in degree from slight innovations to major ones.

Creativity can be viewed both as a mental process and as a result. Ordinarily, a creative process is required to produce a creative result. However, the proverbial monkey at a typewriter might type something that is highly useful and novel without undergoing a creative process. Conversely, by a remarkable act of creativity a young child might produce a result well known to most adults.

---

* This is the title of a book by Alex F. Osborn (New York: Charles Scribner's Sons, 1953) that has been widely cited in connection with application of creative techniques to business.

What mental operations does the brain perform in the creative process? Does it perform special operations that can be characterized as creative rather than analytical? We cannot answer these questions, largely because we cannot observe the creative process directly; its nature must be inferred from indirect clues such as the typical personality traits and thought patterns of creative people or the stages through which creative discoveries commonly pass.

Personality Traits Common to Highly Creative People*

Great creativity is habitual with certain persons; these people are very productive and are the source of many discoveries, not just one. They exhibit a highly organized system of responding to circumstances that is quite unlike that of unoriginal people.

Traits associated with highly creative individuals are independence of judgment, personal complexity, preference for complexity over simplicity, preference for ambiguity over clarity, self-assertiveness or dominance, and reluctance to control impulses. Other traits that often accompany originality include rebelliousness, disorderliness, and exhibitionism.† Of course, some highly creative people lack some of these characteristics.

The Characteristics of Thought Exhibited by Creative People

The chief features of creative thinking appear to be "fluency" (meaning largely the easy retrieval of information from one's memory store); "flexibility" (this trait takes several

---

* This discussion follows the writings of Frank Barron. See especially "The Disposition Toward Originality," *The Journal of Abnormal and Social Psychology*, November 1955, pp. 478–485, and "Originality in Relation to Personality and Intellect," *Journal of Personality*, December 1957, pp. 730–742.

† See George S. Welsh, "Perspectives in the Study of Creativity," *Journal of Creative Behavior*, Winter 1973, p. 235.

forms, including the ability and readiness to reinterpret and redefine information and adapt it to unfamiliar uses and the ability to reclassify and reorder items and thus consider them in an unorthodox light); and "elaboration" (which is mainly related to producing implications — seeing how one item of information implies another).

Another way of defining the abilities most relevant for creative thinking is to group them into two main sets: "divergent production" abilities and "transformation" abilities. The former refers to the capacity to generate large numbers of alternative means for accomplishing a given goal (uncreative people can often think of no more than one way of handling a problem or finding an opportunity); the latter refers to the ability to revise what one experiences or knows in a way that produces new forms and patterns — that is, a capacity for reinterpreting and reorganizing information.*

The Stages through Which Many Creative Discoveries Pass

The stages most commonly distinguished in the creative process include (1) preparation (saturating oneself in the problem; (2) incubation (interruption of conscious effort to solve the problem; (3) illumination (the floating up to consciousness of an essential element of the solution); and (4) elaboration (the process of confirming, expanding, tightening, reformulating, and revising the new idea so that it meshes with what is known and what is needed).† Considerable evidence, based largely on accounts from people who have made major discoveries, shows that these stages usually are present in the creative process; however, they do not always run their course in the given order.

---

* See J. P. Guilford, "Creativity: Yesterday, Today and Tomorrow," *Journal of Creative Behavior,* Winter 1967, pp. 3–14.

† This is the most usual classification and has been proposed by Graham Wallas in *The Art of Thought,* London: C. A. Watts, 1945.

BLOCKS TO CREATIVITY

In general, people greatly underutilize their creative potential. That is not surprising, for many forces conspire to stifle the average person's creativity. The plain fact is that creativity often creates dysfunctional, unpleasant, or obnoxious behavior; those who are troubled by such behavior limit and punish it if they can.

The stifling of creativity begins in early childhood. The average child, even in the most permissive homes, lives in a world of "don'ts." "Don't make things dirty!" "Don't play with your food!" "Don't make noise!" In other words, *Don't do what you want to do! Mistrust your impulses! Be sure that you consider the reaction of mother, father, sister, brother, teacher, preacher, and so on before you do anything!"* These injunctions fill the lives of children and result in a general pattern of constraint—an expectation of objection and a wariness lest one incur punishment.

The influence of early schooling reinforces this pattern with instructions to "speak only when you are called on" and so forth. Some research suggests that the schools act as though they had the fundamental aim of discouraging students' questions by the age of eight. At the age of eight or ten, children ask far fewer questions than they do at the ages of 5 and 6, when they first start to attend school. Up to, say, the level of college, important concern is given in schools to developing self-control, discipline, and the ability to postpone gratification—in general, the ability to refrain from doing, saying, and even thinking things that those in authority consider objectionable.

From elementary school through college, emphasis is placed on logical and careful thought. Precision, accuracy, detail, neatness, organization, and logic are constantly extolled as major virtues, and approval is given to analytical, as opposed to creative, thinking. The preference for the analytical over the creative doubtless rests on many foundations, but the most important is terribly trivial: teachers find it much easier to mark and defend their marks for analytical problems. The scientific method and its associated tradition also elevate analysis over imagination. Indeed, in many cases people exhibit a reaction resembling fear and resentment in response to the brilliant insights of others that seem to be "sheer luck" and frighteningly mysterious.

INCREASING OUR OWN CREATIVITY

It is possible to overcome these blocks to creativity through conscious effort. The first step is to believe we truly possess some creativeness, and the second is to try to be creative—to exercise our creative function. We must expect slow progress when we start to develop our creativity, and we would be wise to measure this progress by comparing our current performance with the results of our initial efforts rather than against our ultimate goal. Much more than our native creative potential, our attitudes and expectations will determine our success in behaving more creatively.

Eventually, through practice, we can train our minds to produce creative ideas—or rather, to let these ideas come through the screening process that has been built up through years of don'ts. Of course, no matter how well our minds are trained, the solutions they produce will be limited by what our minds contain. In other words, the mind must be "prepared" ("preparation" is the first stage in the creative process, as we have noted). It must be fed inputs that it can handle flexibly, that it might transform, that it might pick up, put down, and shift around with fluidity; it must have a wealth of experiences that might be used analogically if it is to achieve major creative results.

To enhance our own creativity, we should adopt a permissive, friendly, and constructive attitude toward the views, statements, and actions of others. Unless we do, we are unlikely to be permissive with ourselves. We should assume that what others say and do has merit, just as our own first thoughts and actions have an underlying reasonableness. We should look for the strong points in the views of others, praise them, and try to extract from them ideas on which we can build. We should resist the impulse to search for their weaknesses.

Such an attitude has effects far beyond the growth in our own creativity; it is likely to increase the creativity of others. By rewarding others' offbeat ideas, we tend to increase the supply of ideas from both others and ourselves. In an environment of receptivity, people will not tie up much energy and attention in erecting defenses against attacks. Also, not finding themselves attacked, they are likely to be far more receptive to what others say.

Creativity comes to people mainly when they are in a constructive, optimistic mood. Depression, anger, sadness, hostility, and the like are inimical to creativity. To put it differently, the tendency to "accentuate the positive" contributes importantly to success, whereas fear of failure increases the likelihood that failure will occur.

Such a permissive attitude toward oneself and others is often hard to develop. Uncertainty is threatening both to people and to organizations, and both people and organizations tend to develop "programs," or specified ways of doing things, that lessen uncertainty and risk. If people are programmed up and down the line, choices are limited, and there is less uncertainty and risk. But there is also less creativity! If you seek creative solutions, you have to be prepared to accept more risk. This means being tolerant of failure. When you ask someone (or yourself) to create, you are asking for a venture into the unknown, and you must allow a greater margin for error; otherwise, fear of failure may hamper initiative.

MANAGING CREATIVE PEOPLE — AND OTHERS

One problem with creative people, of course, is that they can be seriously disruptive to organizations, however charming, amusing, and interesting they may be. A supervisor may appreciate the high creativity of an employee and still debate the wisdom of retaining that person, given the irritations and frustrations he or she occasions. For example, since creative ideas seldom appear exactly at the time they are summoned, the most creative people tend not to conform well to a strict 9-to-5 schedule. They tend to put forth a tremendous amount of effort when they are "hot" or passionately involved in the problem, and then fall into a fallow period; or they may be chronically late but stay longer at the end of the day.

Making allowances for creative people's quirks and foibles will enhance the likelihood that they will be productive, but it may fiercely annoy others who function better in a directive and conformity-demanding environment or feel threatened if someone else seems to be receiving special favors. A supervisor whose department contains both productive conformists and creative nonconformists may expect to have to defend the creative people against the attacks of the more conventional ones — or risk losing the creative people.

Some executives try to steer a middle course. They run fairly directive organizations that emphasize conformity, authority, and reliability, but they establish special arrangements outside the formal organization to generate creative input. Under this arrangement, the creative individuals are isolated from the main body of the business. They can be hired as consultants rather than as employees, or they can be located in an environment carefully designed to foster creativity. Separate R&D departments located far from the home office have been a common feature of large American corporations since about 1950.

This middle course probably works well with research and development—so long as the R&D people are not isolated from the problem itself, in a sort of ivory tower—and perhaps even with editorial and design groups. However, not all business activities that benefit greatly from creativity can specialize the creativity function. Financial planning, for example, offers increasing opportunities for innovative approaches, and these must be developed by people involved in and intimately informed about the financial activities of the firm. Most of an organization's creativity requirements, in fact, must be obtained from creative individuals who work within the regular organization and together with regular employees.

One technique that seems to help in providing a creative climate for *all* employees is to allow space and time for relaxation and/or meditation. Creative solutions, especially the kind that spring from one's intuitive powers, are most likely to be born when the decision maker is in a relaxed state. Transcendental Meditation (TM), once considered a kooky practice inappropriate for business situations, has become increasingly popular in business organizations as well as private homes, and its popularity is bolstered by some statistical evidence from tests and studies.

In one study, the Torrance Test of Creative Thinking was used to compare subjects who had practiced TM for several months with others who were just learning. On all three scales —fluency, flexibility, and originality—the experienced meditators scored significantly higher.* Some organizations now

* Robert B. Kory, *The Transcendental Meditation Program for Business People,* New York: AMACOM, 1976, p. 84.

give their employees "TM breaks" or even sponsor TM training for their employees; however, there are many who say a formal program such as TM is not necessary for a person to reach and benefit from a meditative state. In fact, for some people simple relaxation, coupled with temporary separation from the perplexing problem, helps to attract the creative muse.

Executives need not *be* creative in order to establish an environment in which creativity will flourish. However, they must have or cultivate a taste for the kind of personalities in which creativity tends to be found. And to keep these creative people from going elsewhere, it is necessary to weed out or indoctrinate employees who threaten the permissive climate, and to cultivate in all members of the organization an appreciation of the value of creativity and a willingness to pay the large and strange prices that must often be paid to achieve it.

Techniques for Enhancing Group Creativity

In the business world, as we have noted, most of the work is accomplished by groups and organizations that must, whether they like it or not, work together. And just as it is possible for some people to stifle others' creativity, it is also possible for creativity to be *enhanced* by one's human environment. Sparks from one person's creative impulse can ignite ideas in another person. A "good" group can provide cross-fertilization and also mutual support.

A number of specific tecniques have been developed to spur creative ideas in the business setting. Although many can be used by individuals working alone, they are usually employed in some kind of "creativity session." Some of these techniques can be classified as analytical; others involve free association or analogies. One method — the Delphi technique — makes use of both solitary and group creativity.

Analytical Techniques

Earlier we indicated that creativity is inhibited by the inclination of our society to place emphasis on logical and analytical thought as opposed to freewheeling, unconventional thinking. Certainly, elevation of the analytical over the imaginative can be inimical to creativity; on the other hand, companies can employ several analytical devices to start and direct the *non*analytical process that produces the most creative ideas.

The simplest technique to suggest possible avenues of creative thought is a checklist of questions that directs the thinker's attention to possibilities that might otherwise be overlooked. A simple and quite effective checklist was prepared for this purpose by Alex F. Osborn.* Altered for clarity and brevity, these questions are:

> Can this idea or object be put to other uses?
> Can it be adapted?
> Can it be modified?
> Should it be magnified?
> Should it be minified?
> Can it be substituted for something else, or can something else be substituted for part of it?
> Could its elements be rearranged?
> Could it be reversed?
> Could it be combined with other things?

Naturally, this list, although handy, is not the best set of questions to be asked about any and all problems. Executives would be wise to develop a personal set of questions that fits the situations that arise in their jobs with greatest frequency; these questions should be given to subordinates — either as individuals or in groups — to guide their thinking.

---

* *Applied Imagination*, New York: Charles Scribner's Sons, 1953, p. 284.

Another technique used for generating ideas is attribute listing. By listing all the qualities of the object under consideration and then taking each attribute in turn and trying to change it in all possible ways, one can generate a large number of alternatives. (One might apply Osborn's checklist of questions to each attribute in an effort to consider possible changes.) And putting together combinations of these alternatives can produce a new and different result.

Free-Association Techniques

Free-association methods are intended to produce a ready flow of ideas and overcome blockages that could be caused by critical judgment. A productive free-association group permits no evaluation to be made of any suggestion; ideas that come up are just accepted (others in the group may build on them, adapt them, or ignore them, but they are not to argue against them or point out their flaws). Also, participants are encouraged to produce as many ideas as possible; this emphasis on *numbers* of suggestions helps break down inhibitions. Finally, free-association groups encourage "far out" suggestions.

Generally, free-association techniques generate a contagious enthusiasm. They are fun, nonthreatening, and often generate competition among at least some of the participants to produce more and better ideas than the others. Also, the group can provide stimulation and assistance for individuals who have run out of ideas.

The best-known free-association technique is brainstorming. Brainstorming sessions are fairly short—often less than one hour—and at times are useful even if they last only 10–15 minutes. Usually, participants are not told the nature of the problem before the session. The problem is clearly stated at the start of the session, and the discussion is carefully recorded to ensure that all useful ideas are recalled.

Analogy Techniques

Analogies lie at the heart of most new ideas, for most new ideas really aren't wholly new but are intellectual transplants. Accordingly, a leader of a creativity group will often seek analogies to the phenomenon with which the group is concerned. Several different kinds of analogies have been used, such as personal analogies, symbolic analogies, even fantasy analogies. One kind of analogy technique frequently used in business settings involves "forced relationships."

A forced-relationship process calls for taking items almost at random and then considering them individually in connection with the problem under consideration. For example, if a group were considering a labor morale problem, it might take such unrelated items as baseball, chewing gum, neckties, or foreign travel and answer the question, "What does baseball (chewing gum, and so forth) suggest about labor morale?" This question usually means, What do these have in common and how do they differ, and do these similarities and differences suggest anything that will help with our labor morale problem? Obviously, if a group views labor morale in relationship with such apparently unrelated things as baseball or chewing gum, group members may get ideas that would never occur to them otherwise. Among these ideas there might even be some that are valuable.

It takes little time to apply analogical techniques, and they force thinkers to look for connections in unlikely places. Although the process results in a predominance of chaff, the value of even a grain of wheat is so great that vast quantities of chaff can easily be tolerated.

The analytical, free-association, and analogy techniques described here are usually compatible with each other. An executive seeking a creative solution to a major problem or a new opportunity might conduct many sets of such sessions with different participants.

The Delphi Technique

So far we have described rather simple methods of stimulating creative ideas. Now let us take a look at more sophisticated approaches that have been developed more recently.

One formidable example is the Delphi technique. It was originated by Dr. Olaf Helmer and Norman Dalkey and described in an article published in 1963. Although it was intended mainly for use in long-range forecasting, it is also applied to the quest for creative solutions and for new business opportunities. In the view of its founders, the technique's aim is to "systematically combine individual judgments to obtain a reasoned consensus. Its unique feature and potential merit lie in requiring the experts to consider the objections and concepts of other group members in an environment free from bias caused by personalities."*

The Delphi technique makes use of many experts without requiring that they appear at one place at the same time. Since it is often extremely difficult to assemble a group of experts, for their services are so much in demand, this method offers a substantial advantage. And not only does it avoid the problems that arise from trying to achieve a consensus among people who are in direct personal contact, it also avoids compromise solutions when views diverge; conclusions are not arrived at as the result of specious persuasion by the member with the greatest supposed authority or the loudest voice. Further, the Delphi technique lessens the unwillingness of individuals to abandon publicly expressed opinions.

* Olaf Helmer, "Analysis of the Future: The Delphi Method," *Technological Forecasting for Industry and Government,* edited by James R. Bright, Englewood Cliffs, N.J.: Prentice-Hall, 1968, p. 116. For a detailed description of the method, see Olaf Helmer and T. J. Gordon, "The Delphi Method: An Illustration," in the same book, pp. 123–133.

At no stage in the Delphi technique do the participants meet, though nothing (other than logistics) would prevent a bringing together of the participants after the program has been completed to see whether direct personal discussion adds useful ideas.

The first step is the construction of questions to which the experts are to respond in writing. In the case of a quest for creative solutions, the question might be something like: "What kinds of things that they do not seem to want now will consumers want in this product twenty years from now?" or "In what ways might this product be changed to make it more convenient to use, if one were not at all concerned with cost?" These questions, to which participants are asked to respond with their "first thoughts," invite the conjuring up of alternatives as yet recognized. Participants might be given a few days in which to respond, thus providing time for their unconscious minds to grapple with the subject.

The second step calls for distributing to all participants a summary of all the answers received. No participant is told which of the others made which responses. All are asked to submit additional suggestions and to express their evaluations of the individual suggestions made by the others.

In the third step, the participants' new answers are distributed together with their comments. It is at this point that the participants learn the underlying thinking of the others (though not their identities) as well as their specific answers. The leader of the program is responsible for distilling the responses of the participating experts; the clarity and insightfulness of the leader's distillation will strongly influence the success of the project. The participants are again permitted to revise their answers and are asked for comments.

The final step calls for the program leader to distribute to the participants a review of the comments received, together with the specific answers to the questions raised originally.

The participants are invited again to alter their specific answers should they so desire.

Synectics

This strange word comes from the Greek and means the putting together of ideas or things that do not seem to belong together until after you do it. It is also the name of a company — Synectics, Inc. — that has been conducting research into the creative process and performing consulting and training services for business firms. The people most closely associated with Synectics are W. J. J. Gordon, George M. Prince, and Dean L. Gitter. The firm has issued many promotional documents that describe its techniques, rationale, and some of the results achieved.

The synectics discipline aims deliberately to copy the nonconscious mental activities that occur when people work efficiently and creatively on a problem. It strives to compress these nonconscious activities into a much shorter time span and to force new ideas up for conscious consideration. Synectics is a technique employing a group of participants, but its method and logic can also be used by an individual.

Two basic activities comprise the synectics approach. First, the problem or opportunity under consideration is pulled apart, analyzed, and mulled over to "make the strange familiar." The second basic activity is termed "making the familiar strange." It calls for a determined and conscious effort to achieve a new view of the same old situation and is intended to ensure that participants will not look at the problem in the way that it is usually viewed. (Presumably, almost all the ideas that derive from the prevailing viewpoint have already been exploited.) In the effort to make the familiar strange, synectics practitioners use several different methods of achieving naive or "out of focus" looks at familiar aspects of the world.

The sequence of the synectics approach to creativity is in-

Figure 9. Synectics flowchart.

A. PAG (Problem-As-Given)
This is a general statement of the problem to be solved.

B. Analysis and discussion to make the strange problem familiar.

C. Purge of immediate solutions.

D. PAU (Problem-As-Understood)
An element or aspect of the problem upon which to concentrate.

Analogy Generation — E. EQ (Evocative Question)
A question that *forces* an analogical answer:
1. Direct analogy, or
2. Personal analogy, or
3. Symbolic analogy.

Analogy Development — F. Play with the analogy to understand all its implications.

Analogy Use — G. Application of this understanding to the PAU (or PAG) to see if a new viewpoint can be developed.

H. There are now several alternative courses:
1. If there is a new viewpoint, it should be developed as far as possible and then evaluated.
2. If there is no new viewpoint, another "excursion" is begun to make the familiar strange:
   (a) Make more analogies to the same EQ and repeat F and G, or
   (b) Return to the PAU, use a new EQ, and repeat F and G, or
   (c) If the work in G reveals a new aspect to the problem, state this as a new PAU and repeat E, F, and G.

Source: D. L. Gitter, W. J. J. Gordon, and G. M. Prince, "The Operational Mechanism of Synectics," Synectics, Inc., 1964, p. 14. Copyright © 1964 by Synectics, Inc. All rights reserved.

dicated by the synectics flowchart presented in Figure 9. Observe that four steps precede any conscious effort to seek creative solutions: these are a statement of the problem, an analysis of the problem until it becomes familiar, a review of early "solutions," and a translation of the problem as initially presented into the problem as it comes to be understood by the group at this point. Only when the ground has been prepared in this way do the synectics practitioners begin a directed and concentrated effort to uncover and work with analogies.

Let us define the types of analogies that appear in Figure 9. *Personal* analogy may be regarded as a form of role playing, but with nonhuman entities. Participants speculate on how a particular inanimate object would feel and act in a particular situation. *Direct* analogies are what we ordinarily mean when we speak of "analogies"; they involve things that are like, or have some parallel relationship with, the phenomenon under analysis. In synectics, the direct analogies sought are remote rather than close. For example, for human problems one would seek analogies from the physical sciences; for physical problems, one would look for direct analogies from the social and biological sciences. *Symbolic* analogies are defined as "highly compressed, almost poetic, statements of the implications of a key word in the problem." Some examples of symbolic analogies follow.

Ratchet	Dependable intermittency
Viscosity	Hesitant displacement
Solidity	Enforced togetherness
Forest fire	Progressive ingestion
Machine-gun burst	Connected pauses
Target	Focused desire
Mixture	Balanced confusion
Multitude	Discreet infinity
Acid	Impure aggressor
Receptivity	Involuntary willingness

Once analogies are brought forth, the group is directed to search for connections between analogy and problem. Usually a discussion leader will direct the group's energies to a forced comparison between the analogy and the problem.

As described up to this point, synectics represents an approach that might be used in group creativity sessions that last several hours. (Doctrine holds that no individual session should be prolonged beyond three hours because of the exhausting character of these sessions for participants.) Synectics doctrine has, however, been extended to embrace large-scale, expensive, and long-run business programs for new product developments.*

Neologics

A third formal approach to creativity for business application is termed neologics. It is partly a conscious reversion to the earliest form of thought, *preverbal* thought.† The theory is that modern people are primarily verbal and think in terms of words and symbols; they apparently file their thoughts in brain memory cells on hooks whose barbs are verbal barbs. When we try to solve a problem, we send electrical or electrochemical pulses bouncing around our brains following a logical path of association from word to word and idea to idea. We try to increase efficiency by cross-referencing every word. When we think of the word "bridge," for example, the pulse will hook onto such barbs as dental plate, River Kwai, Toko Ri, George Washington; musicians will have their own version of a bridge.

Although our brains may work in some such fashion, those of our prehistoric, preverbal forefathers could not. They could not file and cross-file their experiences by the use of words, numbers, and symbols. Still, they were forced to solve some very difficult problems before they developed a

---

* This aspect of synectics is developed in detail in W. J. J. Gordon, *Synectics: The Development of Creative Capacity,* New York, Harper & Brothers, 1961.

† This discussion is based on Theodore A. Chesney's symposium lecture notes entitled "Neologics: Theoretical and Operational."

language sufficient to express them. *They filed and cross-referenced by putting their experiences away on hooks with sensory and emotional barbs.* Any particular experience presumably was stored as a memory of what it sounded like, how it looked, in what season it happened, how hairy it was, how soft, how hard, and so forth.

Neologic theory holds that people still continue to file and cross-file on sensory barbs as well as verbal ones, but that they seldom retrieve on that basis. Creative individuals, however, can still sometimes retrieve from their sensory hooks; such retrieval is what is involved in most intuitive thinking. Neologics mainly aims to harness intuitive thinking based on nonverbal retrieval.

Exponents of neologics advance the following general guidelines for the conduct of creativity sessions.

1. *Suspension of judgment.* Every idea has a right to be, though not necessarily a right to survive. Negative criticism has its place, and that is late in the game.

2. *Silence and soliloquy.* In creativity sessions, occasional periods of silence are required during which people can "listen to themselves." Most people benefit from quiet reflection, something that does not occur naturally in a group session. Also, participants in creativity groups are given an opportunity—at least once—to express their views for as long as they desire, with no interruption from the group.

3. *Clearing of the conscious.* After the problem is presented to the group, all participants are asked to express all their immediate thoughts on the matter. All the obvious good and bad solutions thus are brought out into the open at the outset so everyone can relax; their best ideas are already on record.

The processes we have described here can be useful in finding creative answers to both problem decisions and opportunity decisions. Some organizations use these techniques in "one-shot" efforts; they carefully select individuals to work together at some secluded spot under the direction of an experienced group leader, with the specific goal of finding answers to a particular question. A firm might also establish a permanent group (company employees and/or outside experts) whose general assignment is to search out better ways of doing things and better policies for the firm, as well as to grapple with specific problems when they arise.

Whenever people interact personally for decision making, it is important to take account of the mix of people in the group. Studies by the PSI Communications Project at the New Jersey Institute of Technology have revealed that if there is not a true feeling of acceptance and equality among the members of a decision-making group, a "dominance condition" will arise when subconscious or precognitive input is required, and the dominated members will provide incorrect input. As the tests have indicated, the dominated members are likely to be women (in a predominantly male group, but not in a predominantly female group such as the PTA) or sons or sons-in-law of male members of the group.*

Sometimes the dominance is not even that subtle; even in a balanced group there will be some members who will tend to dominate, and the moderator will have to guard against and counteract this tendency. Some executives make it a practice to call on more junior members of the group first in order to avoid their being influenced by the opinions of the senior members.

SUMMARY

Creativity helps executives mainly in uncovering overlooked opportunities and providing novel solutions to con-

* John Mihalasky, "ESP in Decision Making," *Management Review*, April 1975, pp. 32–37.

tinuing problems. Creativity, or applied imagination, is a relatively plentiful resource that lies fallow in most individuals and in most organizations, largely because there are strong forces working to suppress it. Since creativity often creates irritating or confusing behavior, those who are troubled by such behavior try to limit or punish it.

Certain personality traits and thought patterns can be said to be characteristic of highly creative people. Awareness of these characteristics can aid in identifying the creative people in an organization and also in dealing with them more sympathetically.

To increase your own creativity, you can employ two types of self-brainwashing: convince yourself that you can be creative if only you try; and be supportive, tolerant, accepting, reassuring, and optimistic about your own and others' efforts. To produce a climate for creativity in the organization, be tolerant of creative people's foibles and defend them against the attacks of those who are angered or threatened by them. Giving people space and time for relaxation or meditation often helps foster creativity; in order to get a fresh perspective on a problem, it is a good idea to step back from it and relax for a period of time.

Isolating creative individuals from the rest of the organization works mainly in R&D departments; in other parts of the company, creative employees must work right along with more conforming types. Several specific techniques have been developed to capitalize on group synergy in business settings by helping groups of people stretch their collective imagination. Some of these can be employed in "one-shot" creativity sessions, whereas others are best used in regular short meetings over a period of time.

Techniques such as checklists and attribute listing can be used by individuals as well as by groups, although groups are likely to produce a greater variety of ideas. Free-association methods, such as brainstorming, attempt to overcome blocks that may be caused by critical judgment; a good free-association group encourages "far-out" suggestions and generates fun — an element that creative people seem to thrive on. Analogy techniques that force thinkers to look for connections in unlikely places can result in new viewpoints and ideas. Many of these ideas have limited value, but often one grain of wheat among the chaff justifies the small amount of time involved.

The Delphi technique makes use of many experts who do not come into actual contact with each other; it thereby capitalizes on individual as well as group creativity. Two other sophisticated approaches, synectics and neologics, aim to copy the nonconscious mental activities that may occur when individuals are thinking creatively.

10
A PERSPECTIVE

Executives manage decision "factories" that produce business decisions. They will be wise to create at least one production line that identifies potential opportunities and problems; another department will be required to generate signals that a decision may be necessary. With respect to each potential decision executives must then:

1. Make an agenda decision.
2. Consider possible cause(s) of the difficulty.
3. Consider possible remedy points.
4. Develop alternate solutions.
5. Predict the outcomes of the various alternatives.
6. Select the best alternative(s).

This sequence is of course extremely simplified; most decision making is convoluted. The order of these steps is not the same for all decisions, and the same step may occur more than once. For example, predicting outcomes plays a part in the agenda decision as well as in providing the basis for selecting among alternatives.

Then, too, we might add steps to the list. For instance, after the agenda decision has been made, the executive also must decide *how much* time and *whose* time should be spent. The executive cannot study all the problems and make all the decisions personally, so some of them must be delegated. Subordinates must be told how much time and resources to expend on the issue. If the executive elects to send a subordinate to Milwaukee to straighten out the problem, how long should that person stay there, and what should he or she do to solve the problem? Answering such questions is part of the total decision process.

Two other steps should be added to the end of the list: *carrying out the decision* and *evaluating the results of the decision.* Although these steps occur after the decision has been made and thus technically might not be considered part of the decision process, they are nonetheless crucial to the decision. The implementation of the decision is important for an obvious reason: the way in which a decision is carried out can be of greater impact than the decision itself.

Unfortunately, decision reviews are rare. Executives usually breathe a sigh of relief when the decision is made and implementation begins, and they turn to the next problem without providing for a post-decision review. What was learned as a result of the decision is therefore unlikely to be transferred to future decisions, especially if the first decision maker is not the one who will make the decisions later on.

During the decision-production process, a number of ingredients enter into the decision at one or more points. Among these elements are:

- *Objectives* — the organization's ultimate and intervening goals to which decisions are intended to contribute.

- *Models* — the decision maker's image of the situation. This image is composed of facts and theories.

- *Preparedness* — the decision maker's background (experiences, familiarity with the subject matter) and state of mind (relaxed, harried, cautious, and so forth).

- *Creativity* — the decision maker's own inventiveness and/or the results of group ingenuity.

STYLE

Besides these ingredients, other aspects of the decision factory affect the outcome of the decision-production process. These factors are relatively amorphous and may be termed "style." Executives should be aware of their own decision-making style and also of the decision style of the organization in which they work.

What do we mean by "style"? What different decision styles are there? The best way to answer these questions is with some examples.

Executive A is a long-range thinker who likes to look into the future. The view is not too clear out there, but that is what challenges Executive A. He has more variables to play with, and the possibilities intrigue him. He has a high tolerance for ambiguity, yet he likes to organize large numbers of variables. He would rather think about the effects of his decisions over the next ten years than about their effects during the next six months. He would take some short-term risks in the hope of long-term gains.

Executive B, on the other hand, thinks in terms of today and tomorrow, not the next decade. She likes to deal with variables she can clearly see — and those are the variables that go into her tree. She considers how her decision will affect her immediate subordinates and superiors as soon as they hear about it *before* she considers how it will impact on the department over the long haul and thus affect her subordinates and superiors later on.

Then we have the executives C and D. Executive C likes numbers and is quite at home with the more complicated operations research techniques. Weighting variables and figuring out the mathematical aspects of her decisions is like a game to her. Executive D is just the opposite: he would prefer to think his decisions come out of the air or from his muse, and he is repelled by the coldness of mathematical analysis. If he has to use mathematical techniques in his decision making, he delegates that part of the task to someone else.

Organizations may also have styles. Organization W is a small company started by some behavioral scientists, who like to think of their firm as "person-oriented." In this firm, decisions are made by consensus as often as possible, even when this is more time-consuming than having one executive dictate policy. Organization X is older, larger, and structured in a strict hierarchy; no one goes outside the prescribed channels of communication or skips steps in the hierarchy by discussing a problem with someone two or more levels above him. Decisions are made at the top or delegated from the top down, and meetings are used to gather input rather than to form policy.

Organization Y has at its upper levels executives who clearly communicate the philosophy that risk-taking is risky if you want to keep your job. They have developed an entire system of "safe" procedures that have worked in the past, and creativity is not particularly valued. Nor is it particularly needed at this point in the company's life cycle, the top executives feel, for the firm has a comfortable edge on its competitors in the marketplace. They do not feel it necessary to do anything "new" in order to keep that edge. Lower-level managers learn early on that if they never make a mistake, they'll get ahead, so they avoid making mistakes and often make no decisions at all.

Organization Z is younger and tries harder. Inventiveness

is encouraged, for the top executives recognize that to capture an adequate share of the market, the firm must develop
new approaches. Here, failure is tolerated, if not applauded,
as long as the decision maker has proceeded with sound
reasons.

These illustrate a few of the different decision-making
styles one finds in individuals and organizations. Obviously
the styles of our colleagues and our organization affect the
decisions we make. The question "How will my decision be received?" is asked consciously or unconsciously by every decision maker.

Awareness of one's own style is important too. As we have
indicated throughout this book, decision making contains
many unconscious, unpredictable, *human* factors, yet it is possible and desirable to make many aspects of style explicit.
Taking style into account can also improve the quality of
decisions. Suppose, for example, that you know yourself to be
a short-range thinker and that you are called upon to deal
with a problem that involves both short-range and long-range
consequences. In this case, you should include on your decision-making team a long-range thinker who would be sensitive to aspects you might overlook. Or, suppose you are a
"morning person" who gets tired and irritable in the afternoon; the best time for you to make decisions, if you can arrange it that way, is before noon.

WHY DECISIONS ARE NOT AS DIFFICULT AS THEY SEEM

We have tended to stress the complexity of the decision-
making process. Let us turn now to the conditions that
simplify the process in actual practice.

Since all decisions must face the future, they imply forecasts. In the field of business, almost every activity or phenomenon is quite volatile, so forecasts inevitably are inexact.

Moreover, almost everything a firm might do, except for simple matters such as reordering paper clips, has so many consequences that executives are unlikely to recognize all of them. Therefore, the decision maker would be unwise to try to forecast all of them with precision. The gain from a more accurate forecast often may not equal its cost. That is why executives must weigh the costs and benefits of greater accuracy. They must expect to make a certain number of mistakes and recognize that they can avoid them only by never making decisions—which is perhaps the most costly action of all.

Another condition that makes the decision producer's task easier is the fact that some decisions involve only a few of the steps we have listed. In some cases, the sources of a difficulty are well known and the signals are unmistakable; also, certain individuals may have the assigned responsibility of taking care of certain problems. For example, when a machine ceases to function for reasons that have occurred repeatedly and that are expected to recur, the decision maker knows what parts to look at and will administer a policy that dictates who should do what fairly simple operations under specified circumstances.

In other decisions steps can be skipped because the executive can supply inputs from similar decisions made in the past. Models developed in the past to illuminate a process, remedies that worked before, and experiences with some of the causes of difficulties are often transferable. Although in a sense the production process is proceeding in sequence, the executive is not going through each step in detail but, rather, assembling major components from an inventory.

Even without using old models or remedies, an executive can skip certain steps, or parts of steps, in the production process. For example, there may be good reasons for deciding *not* to search for the cause of the difficulty. Also, many decisions are dictated by the calendar or similar cues—they must be made by a particular date—and consequently the signal and the agenda decisions are essentially predetermined.

When executives are placed under such enormous time pressure that it is impossible to collect sufficient information and analyze it, they will often make decisions anyway by some method that probably combines guesswork, the instinctive approach, and creativity that springs from a mind "prepared" by past situations. This kind of behavior is illustrated by the following verse, entitled "A Psychological Tip."

> *Whenever you're called on to make up your mind,*
> *and you're hampered by not having any,*
> *the best way to solve the dilemma, you'll find,*
> *is simply by spinning a penny.*
>
> *No—not so that chance shall decide the affair*
> *while you're passively standing there moping;*
> *but the moment the penny is up in the air,*
> *you suddenly know what you're hoping.**

Finally, responsibility for many decisions is shared. These decisions are divided among the executives of a firm or delegated to subordinates, so no one need carry out all the steps.

How to Be a Better Decision Maker

The following are some suggestions for improving the quality of your own business decisions.

1. Acquire as much knowledge as you can in the areas in which you will have to make a decision. This will improve your chances of having valid models. You will also know more

---

* Piet Hein, *Grooks I*, Garden City, N.Y.: Doubleday, 1969.

about where your best resources for information and help can be located.

2. Know your own style and arrange to balance your own weaknesses. If you need help with statistical areas, for example, make sure it is available to you.

3. Try to make decisions at your best time of day and when you are free from stress. Arrange some "quiet time" in which to let ideas germinate.

4. Approach decisions in a strategic way, making sure all the steps listed at the beginning of this chapter are covered — either performed, delegated, or eliminated for sound and conscious reasons. Quantify those things that are amenable to numerical analysis; recognize that you are measuring the extent to which the decision achieves objectives.

5. Always be on the alert to the opportunity costs of a decision. They are often overlooked.

6. Enhance your own creativity by (1) recognizing that you can be creative and (2) adopting a permissive and constructive attitude toward your own and others' efforts. By accentuating the positive, you will get into an optimistic mood, which fosters creativity and opens doors for others to help you with their own creative input.

7. Don't ignore your hunches, but recognize that your subjective estimates are likely to be off target. Know and allow for your biases.

How to Ensure Better Decisions in Your Organization

Here are a few hints for improving the quality of decisions throughout your department, division, company, or group.

1. Communicate explicitly the objectives of your area of responsibility and relate them to the overall goals of the

organization. Stress the value of capitalizing on the organization's strengths, especially when making opportunity decisions. Select intervening goals and make sure your managers know what they are.

2. For decisions involving difficulties, design a signaling system—a reporting system with appropriate signal levels— that flags only those situations where things are not what they should be.

3. Be particularly careful in the way you deal with your subordinates' mistakes, for that is how they learn whether to take the risk of making a wrong decision. (You are probably communicating this already—in some unconscious way.) If you want more creative decisions, show subordinates that you are tolerant of failure; otherwise they will tend to make "safe" decisions or no decisions at all.

4. Use group problem-solving methods such as free-association and analogy techniques, the Delphi method, Synectics, Neologics—whatever fits best with the given situation and your own managerial style. These methods will heighten awareness of the need for creativity as well as produce ideas that would probably not have surfaced ordinarily.

5. In decision-making meetings, foster a feeling of acceptance and equality rather than competitiveness among the group members. Some members may dominate the group because of their particular personalities, needs, or positions in the company. Guard against this and ensure that the others have their say, otherwise their potential contributions will be blocked, and you may as well not have them in the group at all.

6. Do not criticize offbeat ideas. Rather, see how they can be developed and turned to useful purposes.

7. To encourage creative individuals in your organization, protect them from the stifling effects of conventional

people who resent unconventional behavior. Protect creative people from being overburdened with restrictions. Allow some time flexibility and periods of relaxation or meditation.

8. In building a decision-making team, make sure there is a balance of strengths: long-range and short-range thinkers; hardheaded numerically-oriented problem solvers and unconventional idea people; model builders, computer scientists, and whatever other experts are needed for a particular problem. The decision-making team can even include outside experts when necessary.

9. Be prepared to delegate decisions to others who can make them better than you can. You don't have to be the best at everything.

Appendix A

INGREDIENTS of SIGNALING SYSTEMS

There are four major ideas involved in creating a signal level: (1) random variables; (2) random variation and its measure, the variance or the standard deviation; (3) the two kinds of error (failing to take action when it should be taken and taking action when it is not necessary); and (4) the normal distribution and the central limit theorem.

Statisticians will understand, after reading Chapter 4, how these ideas relate to signal levels. The following description is designed to take the nonstatistician a little further in understanding the procedures involved in building signaling systems.

A *random variable* can assume various values, each with a given (perhaps unknown) probability. The prototype for a random variable is the sum shown by a pair of dice. Here the possible values are any number from 2 through 12, and, of course, in this case we can calculate the probability that any specific sum will occur.

The word "random" represents, perhaps surprisingly, a remarkably complex concept: it is extremely difficult to state exactly what it means to say that something is random. It is most important to be clear that by random variable we do not mean, so to speak, an uncaused variable. However, the number of causes that interact to produce the outcome—the sum in the case of two dice—is so large that we are unable to disentangle them in a way that would permit us to predict the specific outcome of the next occurrence of the random variable. The key, then, to the notion of "random" is the inability to predict a specific outcome of the variable.

A different explanation of a random variable is also useful. In the process of measurement, the random variable is ordinarily called the *error of measurement.* To take the classic example, when an astronomer is trying to measure the position of a star, he invariably finds that different measurements of the position vary somewhat from one another. Clearly, the star is maintaining the same position. So the measurement process is producing measurements that are the true position plus or minus an error of measurement. The error of measurement, then, is the random variable.

This is a useful concept for the case where we are able to predict part of the value of the random variable. In this case we can think of the actual value as being a random variable around the predicted value, in the same sense as the actual measurement is a random variable around the true position of the star.

Either model of a random variable is correct. If we add or subtract a constant from a random variable, we still have a random variable, although it will have a different value from the original one. Therefore, if we are talking about measurements of a star's position, we can refer to the actual measurement as a random variable. But we can also subtract from each actual measurement the star's actual position, at least in theory, and the result is also a random variable, called the error of measurement.

The point of this discussion is that the index number an executive constructs is a random variable, ordinarily around some predicted value. Often the predicted value is the long-run average of the index number in question. Thus, if the proportion of defectives has a long-run average of 2 percent, then the actual daily values of proportion of defectives will be random variables in the neighborhood of 2 percent—if nothing special is wrong with the production process. Again, the regional sales total is a random variable around the long-run average sales total. But if, for example, it is known that sales are always less in July, then it would ordinarily be more useful to consider July sales as a random variable around the predicted July sales.

The second idea we need is the concept of the *variability of a random variable.* Some sets of measurements—for example, precise ones such as the astronomer's measurements of star positions—are likely to cluster very tightly around the true measurement. Other sets of measurements—for example, measurements of television viewing based on small samples— are usually thought of as being somewhat crude. These measurements would differ more widely from each other. Random variables, in short, vary in their variability.

As a simplified illustration, suppose there are two sales regions with the distributions of quarterly sales shown in Table 4. The probabilities are interpreted in the usual way; for example, in Region I we would expect sales to fall between $44,000 and $48,000 about 20 percent of the time. Each of the regions has mean sales of $50,000, but it is evident that

Table 4. Probability distribution for sales levels in two regions.

Region I		Region II	
Sales (in $000)	*Probability*	*Sales (in $000)*	*Probability*
44–48	.2	40–44	.1
48–52	.6	44–48	.2
52–56	.2	48–52	.4
		52–56	.2
		56–60	.1

the two distributions are quite different. The sales of Region I cluster more tightly around the mean than do those of Region II. In other words, the variability of the sales of Region II is greater than that of Region I.

Clearly, variability is important for signaling systems. An index number with high variability might differ quite a lot from the target level, and this would not signify that anything unexpected was occurring. On the other hand, an index number with small variability might differ from the target level by a relatively small amount, and yet this fact might strongly support the existence of a problem.

We need to make these qualitative statements more precise. In order to do so, it is necessary to have a quantitative measure of variability. Introductory courses in statistics discuss several different measures of variability, but the one that is almost always used in practice is the *standard deviation.* The calculations required to obtain the standard deviation of a set of values of a random variable can be found in any elementary statistics textbook. It is sufficient here to state that the larger the standard deviation, the larger the variability and the more dispersed the values of the random variable.

In our two sales distributions discussed earlier, for example, we find that the standard deviation of Region I sales is $2,530 and the standard deviation of Region II sales, $4,380. The size of the standard deviations reflects, as it must, the greater variability of the sales for Region II.

The third idea we need is that of the famous *two kinds of error* which statisticians talk about so frequently and which we discussed briefly in Chapter 4. Basically, one type of error would be to take action when it is not necessary, and the other would be to fail to take action when action is warranted.

For example, let us take the standard control problem of a production line. The line may be functioning adequately, or it may be malfunctioning. The decision may be made to continue the line in operation or to knock it down and look for the cause of the malfunctioning. This gives the matrix in Figure 10.

Figure 10. Error matrix for a production problem.

	Line functioning	Line malfunctioning
Continue operation	Correct	Error
Stop operation	Error	Correct

The decision problem facing the two executives in our Milwaukee example is also of this type. The two possible states of the world are that there really is a problem of declining sales in Milwaukee or that the observed slump is really just a random fluctuation and that there is no problem. The two possible strategies are to take remedial action or not to take remedial action.

This is a decision problem for which there clearly could have been a signaling system. A reporting system for our example would probably have included a breakdown of regional sales by size of outlet. A reasonable signal level would have called attention to the abrupt decrease in sales from smaller outlets. Such a signaling system would have provided the kind of early warning that the two executives in the Chapter 4 dialogue are maintaining they needed.

Clearly, errors of either kind are undesirable, and decision makers would be delighted if they could avoid making any errors at all. Unfortunately, as statisticians are quick to tell us, this is usually impossible to achieve. We need to consider the probabilities with which the two kinds of error will occur. Since the reported measurements are almost always random variables, it follows that there is some probability that any given signal level will be reached simply because of random variation. In the Milwaukee dialog the vice president says that sales for an earlier quarter were 10 percent lower than expected but that Joe Davis, the Milwaukee sales manager, said that this was because some big orders had been delayed. In other words, Mr. Davis claimed that the slump in sales was only a random variation. In retrospect the vice president recognizes that the slump represented a real decline in sales, not a random variation.

If the probability distribution of the reported measurement is known — either from historical data or from estimates of experts — the probabilities of the two kinds of error can be explicitly calculated. Consider, for example, the sales distribution given above for Region I. Suppose the target level for sales in Region I is $50,000, the mean of the distribution. Suppose the signal level for sales in this region is $48,000. This means that if the actual quarterly sales drop below $48,000, this will be called to the attention of the executive as evidence that there is a real drop in sales that may need executive attention. But from the sales distribution we see that the probability is .2 for sales to be below $48,000 simply because of random variation. This, then, is the probability that the signal level will be reached purely because of "chance." If the executive takes remedial action in these chance cases, he will have committed one of the two kinds of error. We can also calculate the probability of the other kind of error, and we will do so shortly.

Since the two errors cannot be eliminated, a reasonable approach would be to attempt to keep the probabilities of the errors at levels that are in accord with the economic consequences of the errors. We will see that this is exactly how a signaling system should be constructed. Before we do this, however, we need some discussion of the well-known *normal distribution,* which is very often used in constructing signaling systems. This, together with the *central limit theorem,* is the fourth and last major idea needed for the creation of signaling systems.

The central limit theorem tells us that whenever a random variable is the sum of a large number of other random variables, then that sum will be, under a very broad range of conditions, normally distributed. Specifically, this means that if we make a large number of measurements of the variable that is the sum, then we will generally find that they conform to the normal distribution. The practical advantage of this knowledge is that it often enables us to deduce in advance the specific normal distribution that will govern the occurrences of some random variable of interest to us.

Consider the total monthly sales of a force of 150 sales people. This value is the sum of the sales of each of the 150 sales people. The sales of each individual sales person is a random variable, and the total sales are the sum of 150 such random variables. Using the central limit theorem, we can conclude that total sales ought to be normally distributed around the "true" value.

Since many indexes used in signaling systems are either totals or means of a number of random variables, it follows that the central limit theorem should usually apply to these indexes. In short, in many cases we will have theoretical reasons to expect the index to conform to a specific normal distribution.

This means that we can often use the normal distribution to calculate the probabilities of the two kinds of error. There are several ways of doing this calculation. It can be done from a distribution based on historical data—whether it is normal or not—or from a distribution based on the judgments of experts. But the normal distribution is a convenient tool, so we will be using it in most of our subsequent discussion.

Executives naturally would like to make the probabilities of the two errors as small as possible. Unfortunately, it is usually impossible to make the probabilities of the two kinds both small simultaneously. Making one probability small usually can be done only at the expense of making the other kind of error have a larger probability.

In order to state the situation more precisely, we need to distinguish two basic kinds of cases; which depend on the nature of the index being used as the basis for the signaling system. In the first case the index has a fixed and noncontrollable variability. In the second case the decision maker has some control over the variability of the index; in particular, the variability can be decreased, although ordinarily only at some cost.

The only way for the executive to decrease the variability of an index is by increasing the number of measurements entering into the index. This usually presupposes that the index is based on a sample of observations and that it is possible to increase the size of the sample. Any index that consists of a single measurement, then, will have fixed variability. Any index based on a sample of observations will illustrate the second case, in which it is possible to vary the number of measurements on which the index is based. (It is not sufficient for the index to be based on an average of a number of measurements. If the number of measurements is fixed, then there is no control over the variability of the index.)

When the variability of the index is fixed (the first case), it is impossible to decrease the probability of one of the two kinds of error without simultaneously increasing the probability of the other. Since errors are often costly, a signaling system ought to minimize the expected cost of the errors that will result from the system. *Standard economic arguments show that this is accomplished when the signal level is set so that the probability of one of the errors times its cost equals the probability of the other error times its cost.* This is the procedure we will follow in determining the best signal level when the variability of the index is fixed.

In the second case, we can control variability by changing the sample size. The effect of increasing the size of the sample is to simultaneously decrease the probabilities of both kinds of error. This, therefore, decreases the expected cost of the errors. However, increasing the sample size always has a cost, and often that cost is large. A standard economic argument tells us that we ought to increase the sample size until the cost of an additional measurement in the sample equals the decrease in the expected cost of the errors that results from using the larger sample. This is exactly how we proceed in determining the optimal signal level in this case.

Signal Levels for Indexes with Fixed Variability

Suppose that for a particular sales region the sales manager expects sales of $50,000 in a quarter. By analysis of past sales in the particular region or of quarterly sales across all sales regions, or by estimates of experts, it is known that the standard deviation of sales is $2,000. We will assume that a normal distribution adequately approximates the sales distribution. How should a signal level be established?

Consider an old-fashioned, hard-line sales manager who might say: "If sales drop below $50,000 in any quarter, I want to know about it immediately, and I intend to shake things up and make sure the sales representatives get back on the ball!"

What is wrong with this approach? It is certainly true that such a policy will ensure that if sales drop below the desired level, the sales manager will consider action. However, this is achieved only at the cost that the sales manager will be "shaking things up" when there is nothing to worry about. We know that 50 percent of the time a random variable that is normally distributed will be below its mean value simply because of random variation. In each such case this sales manager will act as if ordinary random fluctuations are significant when they are not.

Most sales managers recognize that they cannot afford the luxury or cost of shaking things up when there is nothing that needs to be shaken up. What is the alternative?

First, let the sales manager decide the proportion of the times he is willing to undertake remedial action against falling sales in the region when, in fact, the sales are on target within the limits of ordinary random variation. Suppose the sales manager is willing to have one in twenty of his remedial efforts actually be a wild-goose chase. This means that he is willing to have the signal level reached one time in twenty, or 5 percent of the times, as a result of random variation. The remainder of the times that the signal level is reached — 95 percent — will be instances when the sales level is less than the target of $50,000 for good reason.

Since we are assuming that sales are normally distributed and since we know the mean and standard deviation, we can use standard tables of the normal distribution to determine the required signal level. According to the tables, if we set the signal level 1.65 standard deviations below the mean, then there is only one chance in twenty that the measurement will fall below the signal level by chance. Therefore, this would give a signal level of $50,000 − $2,000(1.65) = $46,700. Whenever the index of sales drops below $46,700, the sales manager will assume that this is not the result of random variation.

This procedure could lead to a reasonable signal level—except for one problem: we have ignored the fact that there are two kinds of error, not just one. We did not take into account the other kind of error, which results when the sales manager does not take remedial action because he thinks sales are on target when they actually are below target. With any signal level there is some probability of this kind of error. For example, if the actual sales level has dropped to $46,700, there will be a probability of ½ that the signal level will not be reached. Therefore, there is a 50 percent chance that the sales manager will not consider taking remedial action even though he *should* consider it.

How can the signaling system take the second kind of error into account as well as the first?

Exactly as in the case of the first kind of error, we want to make it explicit so that the signaling system will operate with known and rationally determined probabilities of error. The difficulty is that the probability of the second kind of error will depend on the level to which sales have dropped.

In order to illustrate this, let us use the previously determined signal level of $46,700. Making the reasonable assumption that the standard deviation will remain essentially the same ($2,000), we can use the tables of the normal distribution to calculate some representative values of the probability of the second kind of error (not taking remedial action when it is really needed). This is shown in Table 5, which in-

Table 5. **Probability values for the second kind of error, calculated using the normal distribution.**

Actual sales level	Probability of second kind of error
$48,000	.74
47,000	.56
46,000	.36
45,000	.20
44,000	.09
43,000	.03
42,000	.01

dicates that the greater the actual sales decline, the more likely the signaling system will correctly reflect this fact.

The sales manager must now choose a specific lower level of sales for which the probability of the second kind of error will be controlled. How is he to do this? Usually there is some range of possible levels of sales that are below target but are still tolerable. On the other hand, there is some lower level of sales that the sales manager would definitely consider intolerable and for which he would definitely want to take remedial action. In order to take account of the second kind of error the sales manager must explicitly state the sales level that he definitely considers too low.

Suppose he states that that sales level is $45,000. This means, in effect, that he is saying he is prepared to live with sales that are below target as long as they are in the range from $45,000 to $50,000. It does not mean that he has given up trying to achieve the target level. Nor does it mean that he does not want to take remedial action if sales fall in the "in-between" range ($45–$50,000). It does mean that he is prepared to live with sales in the "in-between" range if random fluctuations happen to work badly against his signaling system.

With the two sales levels—the $50,000 target level and the

$45,000 level of unacceptable sales—it is now possible to take explicit account of the probabilities of the two kinds of error. And we will see that it is not possible to make the probabilities of both kinds of error simultaneously as small as might be desired.

We assume that sales will be normally distributed around $50,000 if they are on target and that they will be normally distributed around $45,000 if they have dropped to this inadmissible level. In either case the standard deviation is $2,000. The two kinds of error result when (1) sales may actually be at the $50,000 level but remedial action is taken; or (2) sales may actually be at the $45,000 level but remedial action is not taken.

For any given signal level we can use tables of the normal distribution to determine quickly the probabilities of these two kinds of error. Thus, for example, we already know that a signal level of $46,700 will produce a probability of .05 of taking remedial action when it is not needed (error of the first kind) and a probability of .20 of not taking remedial action when it is needed (error of the second kind).

But other signal levels are obviously possible. If a larger signal level is chosen, the probability of an error of the first kind will increase and the probability of an error of the second kind will decrease. If a smaller signal level is chosen, the effect is reversed. This is illustrated in Table 6.

How should the signal level be selected? We use a straightforward economic argument. Errors have associated costs: it costs money to make mistakes. If the costs of the two kinds of error are known, then the signal level ought to be determined so that, as nearly as possible, the expected costs associated with each of the two errors are equal.

Thus, in our example, suppose that the usual kind of remedial action includes a number of days of the sales manager's time, perhaps a meeting with the salesmen, and so forth, and that the cost of this is estimated to be typically about $2,000. This is the upper limit to the cost of unnecessarily taking remedial action. There may also be benefits from apply-

Table 6. Calculated probability values for the two kinds of error.

Signal level	Probability of first kind of error	Probability of second kind of error
$49,000	.31	.02
48,500	.23	.04
48,000	.16	.07
47,500	.11	.11
47,000	.07	.16
46,500	.04	.23
46,000	.02	.31

ing remedial action, in that sales may increase even though the action wasn't really necessary. In this case the resulting additional contributory profit of the added sales would have to be subtracted from the $2,000 cost to get the cost of this error. We will assume, however, that $2,000 is the cost of the first kind of error.

The cost of the error of not taking remedial action when it is really needed is likely to be difficult to estimate. It depends on the additional sales that would have been achieved as a result of the remedial action, the additional contributory profit of these sales, the time period over which the additional sales would have been obtained, possible long-range effects (such as loss of goodwill) associated with poor performance, and so forth.

Still, it can be done. For example, presumably the effect of the remedial action will be to raise sales, perhaps to the target level or even higher. Therefore, the discounted value (over a suitable time frame) of the contributory profit of the difference between the target level and the inadmissible level would be a minimum gross return from the remedial action. We will assume that in our example the cost of not taking needed remedial action is $4,000.

Knowing the costs of the two kinds of error, we are ready to determine the optimal signal level. That signal level should be selected which corresponds to the point on the distribution curve such that $2,000 x (probability of remedial action when it is not needed) = $4,000 y (probability of no remedial action when it is needed). This signal level can be determined by successive approximation or by analytical methods that are too complicated to be discussed here. In this case we arrive at a signal level of $47,900. This signal level gives a probability of .147 of taking remedial action when it is not needed and a probability of .074 of not taking remedial action when it is needed. This is the best signal level that can be achieved, granted the subjective estimates and the costs we have assumed.

Admittedly, it can be extremely difficult, and sometimes virtually impossible, to measure the two costs. What should decision makers do then? They must recognize that there is no way to avoid the difficulty. If the costs cannot be estimated by legitimate cost accounting and related procedures, then they must be "guesstimated" by the most qualified persons in the firm. But before we are overwhelmed by the enormity of this statement, we should remember that we always do this kind of guessing; the only question is whether it will be done explicitly, as we recommended, or implicitly, by an imputation argument from any signal level we suggest.

To illustrate the latter option, suppose the sales manager in our example discovers that the costs cannot be estimated in any reasonable way and suppose that he claims he is totally unable to guesstimate them. Nonetheless, he must choose a signal level. Suppose he selects a signal level of $47,000 for the problem as we outlined it above, but without the opportunity costs. We can calculate that this signal level gives a probability of .07 of taking remedial action when it is not needed and a probability of .16 of not taking remedial action when it is needed. But if this is the optimal selection of the signal level, then the expected opportunity costs of the two kinds of error must be equal. Therefore, it follows that his selection of $47,000 as the signal level imputes the ratio of the two costs by the following equation: $0.07x = 0.16y$, where x is the cost of incorrect remedial action and y is the cost of failure to take remedial action when it is needed.

SIGNAL LEVELS FOR INDEXES WITH CONTROLLED VARIABILITY

We have seen that, generally, decision makers cannot make both of the probabilities of error small when the index has fixed variability, as in the sales manager's example. But they *can* when they have control over the variability of the index, although, as might be expected, they must pay for the privilege of doing so.

For any specified sample size the analysis will be exactly as in the fixed-variability example. But in addition we want to balance the cost of a larger sample against the decreased expected cost of the errors that results from using a larger sample with its smaller probabilities of error. The details of the complete analysis are too technical to be discussed here, but the main steps in the argument are straightforward.

As an example we will consider the decision problem of a production line manager regarding the quality of the output of the production line. Suppose that the quality of the line output is measured by the percentage of defective units produced. If the percentage of defectives gets sufficiently high, the line manager will conclude that something has gone wrong with the line. It will then ordinarily be necessary for the line to be shut down and corrective action to be initiated.

Obviously, this is a costly procedure, and it is possible that the manager will initiate corrective action when it is not really needed because random variation has produced a high level of defectives. On the other hand, if corrective action is really needed and the manager does not take it, there are likely to be large costs due to the high percentage of defectives that are then produced. In other words, the usual two kinds of error exist here.

Suppose that the production manager wants the production line to achieve a target level of no more than 4 percent

defectives. (If ordinary good operation, under usual circumstances, produces 4 percent defectives, it is unrealistic and
pointless to establish a target level of less than this percentage
of defectives.) Suppose, further, that the manager has selected 8 percent defectives as the level that is totally unaccept-
able. This means that the manager does not want to take corrective action if the line is producing only 4 percent
defectives; he definitely wants to take corrective action if the
line is producing 8 percent defectives; and while he might
want to take corrective action if the line is producing some intermediate levels of defectives, he can tolerate errors in this
intermediate range.

The index number used in the signaling system for this
kind of problem will ordinarily be based on the number of
defectives found in a random sample of the line output. For
any specified sample size the signal level will be some number
of defectives found in the sample. For any signal level there
will be probabilities of the two kinds of error, and these can be
calculated and presented in a table or as a curve. Unlike in
cases of fixed variability, there will be one such table or curve
for each possible sample size.

Three possible sample sizes might be 100, 150, and 200.
As an example, the numerical values for a sample of 100 are
shown in Table 7. Exactly as for the sales manager's example,
it is impossible simultaneously to make both of the error
probabilities small — as long as the sample size is fixed. However, as the sample size becomes larger, both probabilities can

Table 7. *The two kinds of error for a simple production problem.*

Signal level (number of defectives)	Probability of taking unnecessary action	Probability of not taking needed action
4	.570	.037
5	.371	.090
6	.212	.180
7	.106	.303
8	.048	.447

be made smaller simultaneously. This means that we want to determine not only the optimal signal level for a given sample size but also the optimal sample size.

To establish the optimal signal level for a given sample size, we proceed exactly as in the case of the sales manager's problem. Suppose that the production manager has determined that the cost of taking unnecessary action is $2,000 and that the cost of not taking needed action is $4,000. Consider a sample of 100 items. If we try to equate the expected costs of the errors, we find:

Signal level = 5: $2,000 × .371 = $742; $4,000 × .090 = $360
Signal level = 6: $2,000 × .212 = $424; $4,000 × .180 = $720

It appears impossible to equate these expected costs, because all of the other possible signal levels have a greater inequality than these two. However, it *is* possible by using a device called a mixed strategy. In our case this would mean that 6 would *always* be a signal level and that 5 would *sometimes* be a signal level. Specifically, if the sample has exactly 5 defectives, then a random number is selected and interpreted so that the sample is considered to have reached the signal level with probability .438. This means that 43.8 percent of the samples that show exactly five defectives will be considered to be signals; the others will not be so considered.

This is a mixed strategy, and the effect is to make the probability of the first kind of error .282 and the probability of the second kind of error .141. This makes each expected cost equal to $564. This is the optimal rule for the signal level for a sample of 100.

If the same argument is repeated for a sample of 150, we find that again there must be a mixed strategy. If the sample has 9 defectives, it is always considered a signal, and if the sample has 8 defectives, it is considered to be a signal with probability .603. The expected cost for either kind of error is found to be $423 in this case. This is considerably smaller than the expected cost for the sample of 100, but this is hardly surprising. Obviously, a larger sample gives more accurate information, and hence probabilities and expected costs of error are smaller. But it is equally obvious that larger samples cost more money, and we have not yet included the cost of the sample.

Suppose, then, that the sample cost is $2 per unit sampled. This cost, at least, is usually quite easy to determine. The cost of a sample of 100 is then $200, and the cost of a sample of 150 is $300. We want to minimize total cost of the sample plus the expected cost of the error. We find:

Sample of 100: total cost = $564 + 200 = $764
Sample of 150: total cost = $423 + 300 = $723

Evidently the sample of 150 is preferable to the sample of 100; in other words, the additional information from the sample of 150 is more than worth its cost.

But maybe some other sample size has an even smaller total cost. How can we find the optimal sample size?

The easiest method is simply to use a computer to calculate the total cost for all reasonable sample sizes as we have done for just two sample sizes. This is a trivially easy task for current computers, and it rarely requires more than two or three seconds of computer time.

In this case we find that the optimal sample size is 180. Eleven or more defectives in the sample is always a signal, and exactly 10 defectives is interpreted as a signal with probability .892. The total cost is $716, and no other combination of sample size and signal level has a lower total cost than this. Therefore, the analysis is completed, and we have found the optimal signal level.

The analysis for this kind of decision problem — where there is control over the variability of the index — is not really very much different from cases where we have no control over the variability. The only additional information needed here is the cost of sampling, and this is almost always measurable.

Appendix B

PROBLEMS with EXPECTED VALUE

As we have explained, decision makers seek to evaluate alternative courses of action. That is, they wish to find the alternative that best achieves their set of objectives — say, the one that yields the greatest excess of benefits over costs for a given level of investment and/or risk. Such a process of evaluation rests upon forecasts of each alternative's consequences, which are inescapably uncertain. Accordingly, decision makers must seek a measure for the uncertain outcomes of different courses of action that permits them to be ranked and evaluated. In short, they seek a single figure to summarize the tangible and intangible, favorable and unfavorable consequences, even though those consequences are not known and must often be guessed at.

The device most commonly employed by management scientists to evaluate courses of action is the "expected value." This is computed, as we have seen, by multiplying the value of each possible outcome by the probabilities on the branch leading to the outcome and adding the results. The course of action with the best expected value is selected. Or at least this is the usual procedure. Now we want to raise the question whether this method of analysis is always valid. If it is not, then when is it appropriate to take expected values? And what should be done in cases when the expected-value analysis is not valid? These are the questions we will discuss in this appendix.

It is easy to see that the expected-value analysis is not always valid. In order to show this, consider a simple decision: whether to take a bet or not. Specifically, suppose the decision maker is offered the following bet: an honest coin will be tossed; if it shows heads, the decision maker will be paid $10; if it shows tails, the decision maker must pay $5.

It certainly requires no analysis to recognize that this would be an attractive bet. However, let us construct the decision tree:

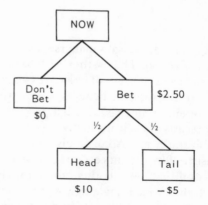

The $2.50 expected value of "Bet" is larger than the zero value of "Don't Bet," so the decision tree analysis confirms the commonsense conclusion that the bet should be taken.

Now let us leave the decision tree as shown but change the amounts to be won or lost. We will change them by multiplying both of them by a constant, so the advantageous quality of the bet will not be changed. Consider a series of possible changes such as:

Win	Lose	Expected value
$ 50	$ 25	$ 12.50
100	50	25
200	100	50
500	250	125
1,000	500	250

This list can be extended as desired, always multiplying the original win and loss by a constant. For every such bet the expected value is greater than the zero value of "Don't Bet," so the decision tree analysis would lead to the conclusion that any such bet should be accepted. Indeed, since the expected value gets larger as a greater amount is bet, it can be argued that the larger bets should be preferred because the decision maker would have a greater total expected value for a series of such bets than for a series of smaller bets.

But is this reasonable? Most people, regardless of the amount of their total assets, will find that in considering this sequence of possible bets, there will be some point beyond which they will not want to take the bet. Thus, one person might be eager to accept the $50-win bet, willing to accept the $100-win bet, dubious about the $200-win bet, and completely unwilling to accept the $500-win bet. This pattern is typical, although the specific preferences will of course vary from individual to individual.

Clearly, this means that the expected-value analysis does not always work since an individual who chooses not to bet in preference to the $500-win bet, for example, is selecting a course of action with a smaller expected value. We cannot say that this is irrational behavior. The only conclusion is that the expected-value analysis is not always correct.

The fact that the expected-value analysis will not always single out the course of action that a rational decision maker will want to follow was first emphasized by Daniel Bernoulli about 250 years ago. The reasons why this is so and what should be done about it have been debated ever since. These questions have turned out to be as interesting as they are important, and there are literally thousands of articles and numerous books devoted to them.

Fortunately, the main strands of the argument that are relevant to executive decision makers can be outlined with reasonable brevity. First we will review the major approaches to the questions, and then we will discuss what executive decision makers should do when they are using the expected-value analysis.

How is the expected value calculated? As we have seen, dollar amounts that are the values of the outcomes are multiplied by probabilities, and the results are added to get the expected value. If in some cases this calculation does not give the "correct" answer, one can say that, so to speak, something is wrong with the calculations. Specifically, something could be "wrong" with the probabilities, with the dollar amounts, with the arithmetical procedure of multiplying and then adding, or with some combination of two or more of the preceding three possibilities.

When Daniel Bernoulli first looked at the problem, he unhesitatingly concluded that it was the dollar amounts — and only the dollar amounts — that were "wrong." This assumption is now called the Bernoulli hypothesis in his honor, and it is the approach to the problem that is the most widely accepted, by a considerable margin.

The point at issue is usually expressed by saying that the dollar amounts do not measure the worth of the dollars to the decision maker. What is necessary, according to Bernoulli and his many successors, is to measure the utility of the dollar amounts to the decision maker. The Bernoulli hypothesis is that if each dollar amount is replaced by its utility to the decision maker and the expected value of the utilities — or the "expected utility" — is calculated, then the decision maker will definitely want to select that course of action with the largest expected utility. In other words, if expected utilities are calculated, there will be no further exceptions to the expected-value analysis.

In Bernoulli's original discussion he argued that the reason why dollar amounts do not measure utility for dollars is because the worth of an amount of dollars to an individual depends on how many dollars he already has. Specifically, the greater the wealth, or total assets, of an individual, the less will be the worth of any fixed amount of dollars. This is certainly at least a reasonable first approximation. In general, people with more wealth often will accept bets with larger wins and losses.

Bernoulli's way of measuring utility used logarithms of total assets. This implies that any differences in individual attitudes toward accepting or rejecting a bet are due solely to differences in the total assets possessed by the various individuals. Two rational people with the same wealth would, according to Bernoulli, always agree in their acceptance or rejection of a bet—or of an investment or a course of action. The modern proponents of Bernoulli's hypothesis believe, however, that there are differences other than wealth which affect individuals' attitudes regarding bets and other kinds of actions involving risk. If this is true, it will be necessary to measure each individual's utility for dollar amounts separately.

Where Bernoulli concluded that it was the dollar amounts that were "wrong," another approach assumes that the method of calculation is insufficient. To make this a little clearer, let us think here in terms of the evaluation of a course of action with many outcomes. This means that we really have a probability distribution of possible dollar amounts. In selecting one of several such probability distributions, the decision maker is expressing a preference for one probability distribution of dollar outcomes over other such distributions. Now, using expected value is equivalent to using the arithmetic mean. Therefore, the expected-value argument is equivalent to claiming that the only difference between two probability distributions of dollar amounts that ought to be considered by a rational decision maker is the difference in their means.

So put, this is a very extreme claim. Any basic course in

descriptive statistics shows that there are quite a few ways in which probability distributions differ other than in their means. They can also differ in their ranges, their variances, their skewness, and so forth. Are these other differences inconsequential for the decision maker? In fact, there is every reason to believe that they are important and should be taken into account. This would suggest that possibly the reason why the expected-value analysis does not always work is that sometimes other characteristics of the distributions of dollar amounts become so important that the decision maker must take them into account.

The main step that has been taken in this direction is the incorporation of the variance of the distributions of dollar amounts in the analysis. This is called mean-variance analysis.* The argument is that if each outcome were certain, the decision maker would simply take the course of action that has the outcome with the largest value. The outcomes are *not* certain, however, for no one knows which outcome will occur. The decision maker wants the greatest possible expected value but is also generally believed to want the least possible risk. Risk is translated as the uncertainty of the outcomes, and some specialists would measure the risk by the variance of the probability distribution of dollar amounts. This means that the decision maker will want probability distributions of dollar amounts with higher expected value and less variance.

The bets we discussed earlier have variances as follows:

Win	Lose	Expected value	Variance
$ 10	$ 5	$ 2.50	$ 62.5
50	25	12.50	1,562.5
100	50	25	6,250
200	100	50	12,500
500	250	125	156,250
1,000	500	250	625,000

* See Harry M. Markowitz, *Portfolio Selection,* New York: John Wiley & Sons, 1959.

It is evident that if the decision maker has a dislike for risk, as measured by the variance, he or she might not want to accept the larger bets. Although there is no generally accepted way in which the decision maker "ought" to combine expected values and variances in reaching a decision, one commonly proposed method would be to use expected value $-$ λ (variance), where λ is determined by the decision maker. The greater λ, the greater the aversion to risk. For $\lambda = .001$, for example, it is easy to calculate that the decision maker would accept any of the bets above from \$10 win through \$200 win but would not accept the \$500-win bet.

The third, and last, approach to this problem that we will discuss here is based on the probability of ruin. Unfortunately, the development of the idea of the probability of ruin involves a considerable amount of mathematics, and the executive would need technical assistance in order to apply it. On the other hand, the basic idea of the probability of ruin is not at all difficult.

Starting once again with the expected-value calculation, the approach based on the probability of ruin argues that the calculations are wrong because they do not take into account the fact that the most advantageous bet, for example, is of no value to the decision maker if he has lost all his capital and can no longer accept the bet. The loss of all capital is what is meant by ruin.

Consider once again the person with \$1,000 capital who is offered the coin-toss bet and who will win \$1,000 if the coin shows heads and lose \$500 if it shows tails. Obviously, in the sense of the usual expected value this is a very advantageous bet. In the long run the bettor could make a lot of money—if there is a long run. In this qualification lies the difficulty. Suppose there is no "long run" for this person, and the advantages of the bet become purely theoretical. This would be ruin for the bettor. Further, if the coin comes up tails twice in a row, the bettor is immediately ruined, so the probability of ruin is clearly at least 1/4. Since this probability is quite large, there would be very good reason for a rational decision maker to reject the bet under these circumstances.

In fact, of course, there are innumerable other patterns of coin tosses that would ruin the bettor. For example, T, H, T, T, T or H, T, T, T, T will also result in ruin. What, then, is the total probability of ruin if the bettor undertakes an indefinitely long sequence of these bets, starting with a total capital of $1,000?

To answer this kind of question requires the mathematical theory of the probability of ruin referred to earlier. In the present case the necessary calculations can be done by hand, but even simple problems usually require numerical methods that are most easily done on computer. In our example, the probability of ruin is .382. This means that if the bettor undertakes an indefinitely long sequence of these $500 bets, starting with a capital of $1,000, the probability is .382 that at some point he will lose all his capital. This is a quite large probability. For comparison, still assuming a total capital of $1,000, here are the probabilities of ruin for some of the other bets:

Win	Loss	Probability of ruin
10	5	0*
50	25	0
100	50	0
200	100	.008
500	250	.146

This approach, then, argues that the decision maker should be cognizant of the probability of ruin associated with bets, investments, or courses of action and ought to control this very important aspect of the risks assumed. Specifically, the decision maker should establish what is an "acceptable" probability of ruin, and all courses of action that exceed this prob-

* The zero probabilities of ruin are not actually zero, but they are all less than 1 in 10,000.

ability of ruin should be eliminated. Then the decision maker can choose the course of action with the largest expected value from among those that meet the established requirements on the probability of ruin.

These, then, are the most important factors to be considered when there is reason to be dubious about the expected-value analysis. Which approach should we use in making decisions? When? How should we proceed in our analysis of the decision tree?

Earlier we used bets to show that the expected-value analysis does not always produce conclusions that are in accord with the commonsense preferences of rational decision makers. But obviously, the same situation can arise when the comparison is among courses of action in decision problems. All that is needed for the question to arise is the possibility of significant losses or costs that may make the decision maker dislike a given course of action despite its attractive expected value. How is such a situation to be recognized? And how often does it occur? Our emphasis on the usefulness of the expected-value analysis would be rather misplaced if it turned out that most of the time some other analysis must be used.

Fortunately, this is not the case. For the great majority of decision problems the expected-value analysis is all that is needed. The occasions when the expected-value analysis must be questioned are suggested by the phrase in the preceding paragraph: "the possibility of significant losses or costs."

The important word here is "significant." Losses or costs are significant when they represent a major proportion of wealth or total assets. When the maximum possible loss or cost from a course of action is an insignificant proportion of total assets, then expected-value analysis can be used with no hesitation whatsoever. "Insignificant" can be defined as less than 2–3 percent of total assets. Whenever the maximum amount of possible loss or cost is less than that proportion, then the expected-value analysis is all that is needed. (This can be shown to be a reasonable rule by mathematical analysis, by introspection, and by laboratory experiments.) Since the overwhelming proportion of corporate decision problems meet this requirement, it follows that the expected-value analysis is sufficient most of the time.

Therefore, one way of recognizing that a decision problem may not be satisfactorily analyzed by calculating the various expected values is that the largest amount of possible loss or cost is greater than 3 percent of total assets. There is another symptom of the possible inappropriateness of expected values that is worth noting. This arises from the distinction between opportunity costs and out-of-pocket costs.

As an example, consider the decision to market or not to market a new product. Suppose for simplicity that there are just two states of the world — low demand and high demand — and that the only question at issue is whether or not to build a $500,000 plant to produce the new product. Suppose the discounted values of the contributory profits of the two states of the world are $200,000 and $1,000,000, respectively. A simple way to express the values of the outcomes would be as opportunity costs. If the product is marketed, there is no opportunity cost if demand is high, because this was the best possible course of action. But if demand is low, there is an opportunity cost of $300,000, because this amount would have been saved by not marketing. Similarly, the opportunity cost of not marketing if demand is high is $500,000, the amount that would be foregone because the product was not marketed. Finally, if the probability of high demand is estimated to be .5, the decision tree looks like Figure B1.

The decision should be to market since an expected opportunity cost of $150,000 is better than an expected opportunity cost of $250,000.

At this point the decision maker may have second thoughts about our analysis. He might say, for example, that the $300,000 cost of marketing when demand is low is an out-of-pocket cost that must be paid out by the company whereas the $500,000 cost of not marketing when demand is high is only contributory profit not made. The decision maker may

Figure B1. Decision tree for a marketing problem.

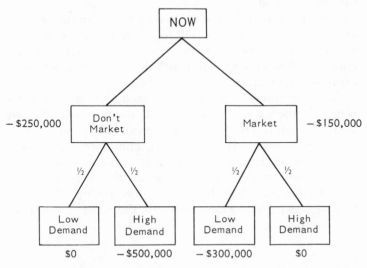

Figure B2. Alternative decision tree for the marketing problem.

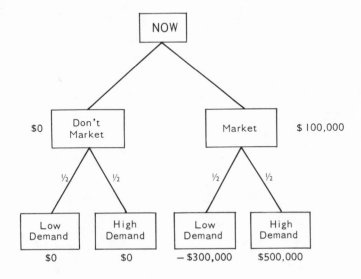

maintain that he does not consider these costs to be directly comparable at all.

Now, there is nothing whatsoever wrong with the decision maker's logic in such a case, but his argument is incompatible with the use of expected values. To see this in our example, Figure B2 shows the same tree with the value of the outcomes expressed as changes in assets.

The conclusion is still that the product should be marketed. Further, it can be shown that the results of the two analyses — in terms of changes in assets and in terms of opportunity costs — will always be identical. Therefore, if a decision maker believes that out-of-pocket costs and opportunity costs are not comparable, it follows that for that person the expected value analysis is dubious. In most business decisions, however, expected-value analysis is the most appropriate procedure.

Appendix C

DECISION-TREE ANALYSIS— AGENDA DECISION

Let us now develop the decision-tree analysis for the agenda decision of the Milwaukee example. This analysis ought to be done by the vice president since it is his agenda decision.

Several possibilities were suggested in the dialog. First, there has been a sales slump in the small retail outlets, and there is strong evidence that this is the fault of the distributor. Second, there is a possibility that the slump is due to competitive price cutting, which probably is not the fault of the distributor.

Third, if the distributor is at fault, it may be the result of some temporary personal problems. Fourth, there is a possibility that the distributor has undergone some major psychological change, which is resulting in his poor performance—assuming that he is actually performing poorly. Fifth, if the distributor is not doing his job, it may have compromised his relationship with the small retailers so severely that the company's position with them cannot be reestablished without changing the distributor.

What, then, are the actions available to the vice president?

We will simplify somewhat by ignoring the possibility that he might assign an assistant to the problem. Instead, we will assume that the question is whether the VP himself should devote time to the problem. Obviously, one course of action is to replace the distributor without any further investigation. Another possible course of action is to devote some time to an investigation of the problem. What may the VP discover, and what further courses of action will be available to him?

We can safely assume that if the problem is really due to competitive price cutting, the VP will find this out in his on-the-scene investigation. Suppose, then, that the distributor is really performing poorly. Apparently, any explanation of his behavior is irrelevant if his relationship with the small retailers has been compromised beyond redemption. In this case, both executives agree, he must be replaced. But if this is not so, then it may be that his behavior can be corrected.

One possibility is that it is just some kind of temporary dereliction. We will assume that in that case the vice president might do something like having a serious talk with the distributor, which would be sufficient to get him to function again. If this is so, then the VP might temporarily assign an extra person to the sales region to help regain the former position with the small retailers.

The other possibility is that the distributor has undergone a major psychological change. The VP has indicated that he has little interest in attempting "psychoanalysis," but we will assume that he recognizes that a person might have some psychological problems that need not adversely affect his performance if he is given some counseling or training. We will further assume that the VP believes he will recognize whether such an approach will work and, if this is the case, that he will also temporarily assign an extra person to help reestablish the company's position with the small retailers. This exhausts the possibilities mentioned in the discussions the VP had with the Milwaukee sales manager and other people.

We are now ready to draw the skeleton of the decision tree (see Figure C1). The relevant states of the world are that ei-

Figure C1. Decision-tree skeleton for the Milwaukee problem.

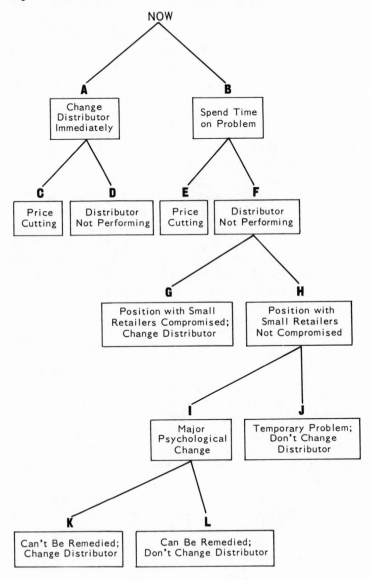

ther there is price cutting or the distributor is performing poorly. Since, in decision trees, states of the world (variables over which the decision maker has no control) are treated as outcomes, we put the states of the world immediately under the first courses of action. The rest of the tree exactly follows our discussion of this case. (To facilitate the subsequent discussion, the various nodes of the tree are designated by letters.)

Next we need the costs. We learned from the discussions that the cost of changing the distributor is $40,000. This is the cost for node D in Figure C1. We will assume that the vice president's salary is $100,000 per year. He estimates that a trip to Milwaukee will require one week of his time. This is about $2,000 in salary, and we arbitrarily and and optimistically (on the grounds that he is expected to make twice as much for the company as the company will have to pay him in salary) multiply by two to get an estimate of the value of his time to the company. Suppose the out-of-pocket costs of a one-week trip are $1,000. Then the cost of the VP's devoting one week to this problem is $5,000. This means that the costs for nodes G and K are each $45,000 ($40,000 to change the distributor plus $5,000 for the VP's week on the problem).

Suppose the vice president estimates the cost of the additional person he will assign (nodes J and L) as $10,000. Then the cost for node J is $15,000. He estimates the cost of sending the distributor for appropriate psychological training (node L) as $5,000. Then the cost for node L is $20,000 ($10,000 for the additional person, $5,000 for the vice president's time, and $5,000 for the psychological training).

We still need the costs for nodes C and E. Clearly, if price cutting is the problem, the VP will take some action, and this will cost some amount. But note that we do not need to include that among the costs for C and E. Whatever this cost is, it will affect the two nodes equally. All we need is the differential costs in the two cases. This means that the cost for E is simply the $5,000 cost of the vice president's time. Node C will have the $40,000 cost of replacing the distributor plus a cost due to the fact that it will then be a much longer time before it is clear that the problem is really one of price cutting. If the vice president estimates this additional cost at $25,000, it follows that the cost for C is $65,000.

Now we need the probabilities. First, what are the probabilities of the two states of the world? As we have seen, the vice president has made it clear that he is very doubtful that the problem is due to price cutting. Suppose, then, that he estimates that the probability is .1 that price cutting is the true cause of the problem. Most executives have a sufficiently good understanding of probabilities to distinguish a probability of one in a hundred (.01), one in twenty (.05), one in ten (.1), and so forth. And this is often sufficient for initial estimates. The .1 applies, then, to both nodes C and E, and .9 applies to nodes D and F.

What is the probability that the distributor's position with the small retailers has been compromised? Presumably the vice president has had some experience of the effect of a neglectful distributor on retailers. Suppose that he estimates that the probability is .5 that the distributor's position is compromised. Then the probability of node G is .5, and the probability of node H is also .5, by subtraction from 1.

Let us now proceed down the tree. The VP has stated that he has some reason to suspect that the distributor has undergone a major psychological change. If he does not feel very strongly about this, he might estimate the probability of node I to be .6; hence the probability of node J would be .4. Finally, the VP has expressed considerable scepticism about the possibilities of psychological counseling. Suppose, therefore, that he estimates the probability of node K to be .9 and the probability of L to be .1. This completes the tree; the result is as shown in Figure C2.

The expected values of the other nodes are calculated in the usual way, moving up the tree from the bottom to the top. They are shown in parentheses. Thus the expected value for node I is $42,500 = .9 (45,000) + .1 (20,000), and for node H, $31,500 = .6 (42,500) + .4 (15,000). It can be seen that the ex-

Figure C2. Completed decision tree for the Milwaukee problem.

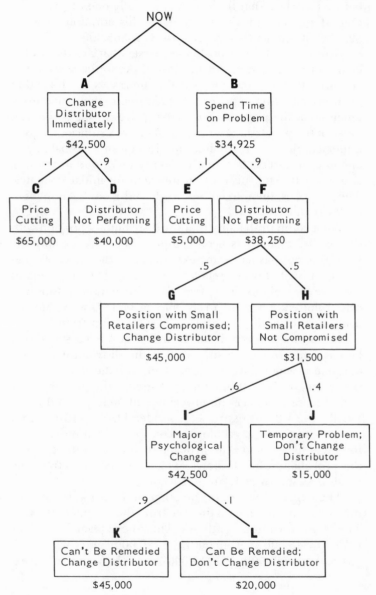

pected cost of $34,925 for node B is considerably lower than the $42,500 expected cost of A, so the conclusion is that the vice president ought to devote a week to this problem.

We have assumed in this analysis that the vice president does have time available for the Milwaukee problem if it is worthwhile. In one of the discussions he said he needed all of his time for a different problem (a strike in Peoria). If that is the case, then the tree can be constructed to represent this use of his time as well. However, it is more likely that if the analysis of the Peoria problem promised a higher return for his time, the VP would either assign an assistant to the Milwaukee problem or simply postpone action on the Milwaukee problem until he was finished with Peoria. In any case, no useful purpose would be served here by adding these various possibilities to our decision tree.

This whole analysis would take no more than a few hours to do. Surely the return in clarity concerning the decision problem amply justifies the expenditure of so little effort.

INDEX